FLOYD CLYMER'S MOTORCYCLIST'S LIBRARY

The Book of the
NSU PRIMA

BY

R. H. WARRING

ANNOUNCEMENT

By special arrangement with the original publishers of this book, Sir Isaac Pitman & Son, Ltd., of London, England, we have secured the exclusive publishing rights for this book, as well as all others in THE MOTORCYCLIST'S LIBRARY.

Included in THE MOTORCYCLIST'S LIBRARY are complete instruction manuals covering the care and operation of respective motorcycles and engines; valuable data on speed tuning, and thrilling accounts of motorcycle race events. See listing of available titles elsewhere in this edition.

We consider it a privilege to be able to offer so many fine titles to our customers.

FLOYD CLYMER
Publisher of Books Pertaining to Automobiles and Motorcycles

2125 W. PICO ST.   LOS ANGELES 6, CALIF.

INTRODUCTION

Welcome to the world of digital publishing ~ the book you now hold in your hand, while unchanged from the original edition, was printed using the latest state of the art digital technology. The advent of print-on-demand has forever changed the publishing process, never has information been so accessible and it is our hope that this book serves your informational needs for years to come. If this is your first exposure to digital publishing, we hope that you are pleased with the results. Many more titles of interest to the classic automobile and motorcycle enthusiast, collector and restorer are available via our website at www.VelocePress.com. We hope that you find this title as interesting as we do.

NOTE FROM THE PUBLISHER

The information presented is true and complete to the best of our knowledge. All recommendations are made without any guarantees on the part of the author or the publisher, who also disclaim all liability incurred with the use of this information.

TRADEMARKS

We recognize that some words, model names and designations, for example, mentioned herein are the property of the trademark holder. We use them for identification purposes only. This is not an official publication.

INFORMATION ON THE USE OF THIS PUBLICATION

This manual is an invaluable resource for the classic motorcycle enthusiast and a "must have" for owners interested in performing their own maintenance. However, in today's information age we are constantly subject to changes in common practice, new technology, availability of improved materials and increased awareness of chemical toxicity. As such, it is advised that the user consult with an experienced professional prior to undertaking any procedure described herein. While every care has been taken to ensure correctness of information, it is obviously not possible to guarantee complete freedom from errors or omissions or to accept liability arising from such errors or omissions. Therefore, any individual that uses the information contained within, or elects to perform or participate in do-it-yourself repairs or modifications acknowledges that there is a risk factor involved and that the publisher or its associates cannot be held responsible for personal injury or property damage resulting from the use of the information or the outcome of such procedures.

WARNING!

One final word of advice, this publication is intended to be used as a reference guide, and when in doubt the reader should consult with a qualified technician.

PREFACE

THE motor-scooter is a vehicle which has become completely accepted as a logical, safe, reliable and very inexpensive method of transport for the owner-driver. It is a class of vehicle on its own, developed and popularized in Continental Europe in the years following World War II, a time when roads were poor and travel had to be really cheap to attract potential buyers.

By cheap travel we refer specifically to operating costs. The initial cost of a motor-scooter is not low, and is directly comparable with a motor-cycle. From a production point of view it is every bit as complicated as a motor-cycle, a fact which largely accounts for its price. The scooter is not just an "adaptation," but a specialized design which aims at getting the best possible performance out of an engine of modest size and power output. It is in this small size of engine that the economy of running arises.

Reliability is of the highest order—from a scooter of reputable make—always provided that the machine is properly looked after. The rise in popularity of this type of vehicle has led to dozens of different makes of scooters appearing on the market—the leading brands outstanding in all respects, others ranging from good to indifferent, to downright poor.

The NSU Prima stands right at the top as regards reliability and quality production. It is a machine which has been extensively developed, first by experience in manufacturing the Italian Lambretta under licence in Germany, followed by variants on the original designs and finally an entirely new design throughout which was originally introduced in this country as the Prima "Five Star."

Although all Primas are manufactured in Germany, the British company responsible for their import and distribution—NSU (Great Britain) Ltd.—is organized to deal with all owner demands in regard to spares and servicing; the latter are normally carried out by the range of NSU accredited dealers throughout the country. Ownership of a "foreign made" machine, therefore, implies no difficulty in obtaining spares or specialized service and, after overcoming initial difficulties in the early days, NSU service is, in fact, probably better than that for some British products. And certainly the tens of thousands of Primas on the roads of this country underline the fact that it is one of the "accepted" types.

In preparing this book for the Prima owner-driver the writer is very much indebted to NSU (Great Britain) Ltd., both for assistance readily

PREFACE

given in preparing the text in accordance with the techniques recommended by them and for the instruction and help always willingly given on the various visits made to their works. Appreciation is also due to the parent company for permission to use and adapt many of the illustrations used, particularly those of component assemblies, etc.

R. H. WARRING

BECKENHAM
1960

CONTENTS

PAGE

CHAP.
I. THE PRIMA MODELS 1
II. BASIC DESIGN AND LAYOUT 7
III. OPERATION AND HANDLING 18
IV. REGULAR MAINTENANCE 32
V. TRACING AND CURING FAULTS 41
VI. DETAILED MAINTENANCE (GENERAL) 45
VII. PRIMA D ENGINE UNIT 63
VIII. PRIMA D, FURTHER DETAILS 70
IX. PRIMA V AND III ENGINE UNIT 76
X. PRIMA V AND III, FURTHER DETAILS 84
XI. THE DYNASTART UNIT 90
XII. IGNITION AND LIGHTING 94
Index 101

CHAPTER I

THE PRIMA MODELS

NSU, NAMED after the south German town of Neckarsulm where the factory is situated, are Germany's largest manufacturers of mopeds, motor-scooters and motor-cycles. The origin of the company dates back to the last century when they took a pioneering interest in the internal combustion-engine-propelled vehicle, and prior to that they were manufacturers of sewing machines on a considerable scale. The present factory is entirely modern, having been completely rebuilt after World War II, and is equipped throughout with the latest types of machine tools, production lines and finishing equipment, etc.

Post-war production restarted with motor-cycles, which are currently still a major item, alongside mopeds, scooters and small cars. The first scooter to be produced was the 125 c.c. Lambretta, manufactured under Italian licence. A 150 c.c. Lambretta followed, both being marketed in Germany under the name NSU Lambretta.

With the cessation of this licence contract NSU introduced their own 150 c.c. scooter, essentially similar in design to the Lambretta LC, and called the "Prima." A version of this known as the Prima D came out in early 1956 and became available on the British market the same year through NSU (Great Britain) Ltd. (*see* Fig. 2).

In 1958 an entirely new design was introduced, originally designated the Prima Five Star but later, and more correctly, known as the Prima V. The Prima V, far from being a development of the Prima D, can only be described as an entirely new design. The new 175 c.c. engine was side mounted with the gearbox drive coupling directly to the rear wheel instead of via a drive shaft; the gearbox incorporated four forward speeds instead of three with a footchange action instead of twist-grip gear change; wheel diameter was increased to 10 in. (from 8 in.); there are entirely different front forks; and other differences throughout. Outwardly, however, when the covers are in place these major differences may not be apparent at first except for the difference in grille and motifs, although here again there is more than a superficial change. The Prima V covers consist, basically, of two half shells mounted around the engine and rear unit. The Prima D fairings comprise a centre section panel, a separate rear section (rear mudguard, in effect), plus two separate side panels.

The Prima V (Fig. 1) is essentially a de luxe motor-scooter, complete with self starter and embodies in its 175 c.c. engine about the maximum power normally considered advisable for this class of vehicle. Absolute top speed is of the order of 55–60 m.p.h. with excellent acceleration and good hill-climbing capabilities.

A further variant of this design was introduced in 1959, designated the Prima III—virtually the same machine throughout except that engine capacity was lowered to 146 c.c. by reducing the bore and the gearbox to rear wheel gear ratio was modified to accommodate the reduced power and still retain satisfactory acceleration.

Of the three variants of the Prima III which have appeared, only the Prima III KL has been imported into this country for general distribution.

Fig. 1. NSU "Five Star" Prima Introduced in 1958 Represented an Entirely New Design Throughout. Subsequently Known as the Prima V

The Prima III version is basically as the Prima V, with the smaller engine but retains 12-volt electrics and a self-starter motor. The Prima III K dispenses with the Dynastart in favour of a kick starter and utilizes 6-volt electrics. Chrome and general trim are also reduced to provide a "minimum cost" machine in this category. The Prima III KL can be described as a de luxe version of the III K, reverting to a kick starter and 6-volt electrics but with a certain amount of the trim and chrome replaced (*see* Figs. 7 and 16).

From the point of view of general operation and routine maintenance, all the Primas can be regarded as of a similar type, except where specific differences exist (i.e. in the gear change between the Prima D and the Prima V and III). The handling of all models is therefore discussed together under the appropriate chapters, with such specific differences duly noted.

From the engineering standpoint, however, whilst the Prima V and Prima III are basically the same, the Prima D is entirely different throughout. For the purpose of describing detailed maintenance, therefore, they are treated as separate machines and only the appropriate sections apply to a particular model.

All NSU Prima scooters distributed in this country are imported by a British company—NSU (Great Britain) Ltd.—with registered offices at 7 Chesterfield Gardens, Curzon Street, London, W.1. This company was established in 1954 and also operates an extensive maintenance and spares section at 136 King Street, Hammersmith, London, W.6, to handle major overhauls and repairs and the distribution of spares and service recommendations to accredited NSU agents and dealers throughout the country. In addition the Hammersmith section runs a school for dealers, giving practical instruction and up-to-date experience with all types of NSU machines so that, although the origin of manufacture is outside this country, complete liaison is maintained between manufacturer, distributor and dealer or agent in contact with the private owner.

All authorized NSU agents and dealers carry a representative selection of spares and special tools to facilitate servicing as part of their agency agreement. Recommended practice is, therefore, for private owners to deal with NSU agents for all requirements. All NSU spares are manufactured in Germany and many components, such as nuts, screws, etc., are of German DIN standard which is different from English standard threads normally stocked by garages.

Normal routine maintenance and adjustment of a straightforward nature should be well within the capabilities of any owner, however lacking in previous experience in engineering matters, for it is basically simple and logical. More detailed maintenance can also be tackled by following the stripping and reassembling instructions given in later chapters.

It can be emphasized that often the major charge in the case of a professional repair is associated with labour time rather than material costs. To the private owner who can develop a flair for looking after his machine time is free and considerable cash savings can result, if he is prepared to do his own maintenance work.

TECHNICAL DATA, PRIMA D

Engine: type 11/150 c.c. NSU-Scooter, single cylinder two-stroke; bore 57 mm; stroke 58 mm; displacement 147 c.c.; compression ratio 6·3:1; maximum power 6·2 b.h.p. at 5,000 r.p.m.

Carburettor: Bing 1/20/22—main jet No. 120 or 95 (depending on silencer fitted); needle jet 2·68; needle position No. 2 groove; slow running jet No. 45.

Bing 1/20/37—main jet No. 90; needle jet 2·68; needle position No. 2 groove; slow running jet No. 45.

Ignition: timing $\frac{5}{32}$ in. before T.D.C.; contact-breaker gap 0·016 in. (fully retarded position); spark plug Bosch W 240 T 11[1]—gap 0·028 in.; 12-volt d.c. coil ignition from Dynastart unit.

Transmission: NSU 3-speed gearbox; engine–gearbox drive—spiral bevel gears; gearbox–rear wheel drive—shaft drive with spiral bevel gears and spur gears with straight teeth; engine:gearbox ratio 1·3125:1; ratio of gears, 1st gear 2·96:1, 2nd gear 1·46:1, 3rd gear 1:1; gearbox: rear wheel ratio, 1st gear 14·66:1, 2nd gear 7·259:1, 3rd gear 4·948:1.

Clutch: multi-plate type in oil bath; clutch spring pressure 137 lb; clutch adjustment $\frac{3}{16}$ in.–$\frac{5}{8}$ in. play between lever and clutch cover.

Wheels: 2·45–8 DIN 7824 well base.

Tyres: 4·00 × 8.

Brakes: internal expanding shoes, mechanically operated.

Dimensions: wheel base 49·6 in.; overall length 75 in.; overall width 26·6 in.; overall height 38·2 in.; ground clearance 5·5 in.; saddle height 31·2 in.

Weights: unloaded (with fuel) 270·5 lb; maximum permissible total load 660 lb.

Fuel capacity: 21 pints (including 2¼ pints reserve).

TECHNICAL DATA, PRIMA V

Engine: type 28 NSU single cylinder, two-stroke; bore 62 mm; stroke 57·6 mm; displacement 174 c.c.; compression ratio 6·35:1; power 9·3 b.h.p.; maximum r.p.m. 5,100.

Carburettor: Bing 1/24/109 (up to model 2 206 067/3 456 233); main jet 105; slow running jet 50; starter jet 90; needle jet 16·08; throttle valve No. 4; jet needle No. 3; needle position 2; idling screw 1½ turns open.
   Bing 1/24/112 (from 2 206 068/3 456 234 onwards) main jet 105; slow running jet 40; starter jet 90; needle jet 16·08; throttle valve No. 4; jet needle No. 3; needle position 2; idling screw 1 turn open.

Ignition: timing 0·177 in. before T.D.C.; contact-breaker gap 0·012 in–0·015 in.; spark plug Bosch W 190 M 11 S[2]—gap 0·020 in.–0·024 in.; 12-volt d.c. coil ignition from Dynastart unit (Prima V).

[1] *See* Chapter VI for British equivalents.
[2] *See* Chapter VI for British equivalents.

THE PRIMA MODELS

TECHNICAL DATA, PRIMA III K and III KL

Engine: NSU single cylinder, two-stroke; bore 57 mm; stroke 57·6 mm; displacement 146 c.c.; compression ratio 6·5:1; maximum power 7·4 b.h.p.; maximum r.p.m. 5,100.

Carburettor: Bing 1/22/105; main jet 105; needle jet 16·08; needle position 2; slow running jet 40; starter jet 90; idling screw 1 turn open.

Ignition: timing 0·16 in. before T.D.C.; contact-breaker gap 0·012 in. to 0·015 in.; spark plug Bosch W 190 M 11 S[1]—gap 0·020 in–0·024 in.

Ignition: flywheel magneto.

Lighting: 6-volt 6·7 amp-hour battery.

GENERAL SPECIFICATION, PRIMA V and III

Transmission: NSU foot-operated 4-speed gearbox.

Ratio of gears—	Prima V	Prima III
1st gear	3·25:1	18·01:1
2nd gear	2·19:1	10·86:1
3rd gear	1·6:1	7·72:1
4th gear	1·17:1	5·65:1
Gearbox:rear wheel ratio	4·14:1	4·14:1

Clutch: single plate; clutch adjustment 2–3 mm (0·008 in.–0·012 in.) play on clutch throwout lever.

Wheels: well base rim 2·50 in. × 10 in.

Tyres: 3·50 × 10.

Brakes: internal expanding shoes, mechanically operated.

Dimensions: wheel base 48½ in., overall length 75 in., overall width 25·625 in., overall height 30·75 in., ground clearance 5 in.

Weights: loaded (tank full) 304¼ lb; maximum permissible loaded weight 661 lb.

Fuel capacity: 2·9 gallons (including 3¾ pints reserve).

Maximum speed: Prima V, 55 m.p.h. (approximately); Prima III KL, 50 m.p.h. (approximately).

[1] *See* Chapter VI for British equivalents.

Fuel consumption: Prima V, 85–90 m.p.g. (approximately); Prima III KL, 100 m.p.g. (approximately).

Colour schemes: Prima D: light blue; Mitra red; jade green; black.

Two-tone: pillarbox red/off white; black/lime green; turquoise/ivory.

Prima V: Sahara beige; delphinium blue; brick red.

Prima II KL: turquoise/ivory; black/lime green; pillarbox red/off white.

The above refer to original colour schemes as introduced on the various models up to 1960.

CHAPTER II

BASIC DESIGN AND LAYOUT

THE Prima D features a single cylinder air-cooled two-stroke engine operated on a 20:1 to 25:1 petrol-oil mixture with ignition provided by a flywheel magneto. The latter also includes a dynamo circuit for battery charging—*see* Chapter IX—and provision for operation as a starter motor. Standard instruments comprise an illuminated speedometer in which is mounted a fuel-supply warning light and an ignition warning light. There is a combined starter, ignition and lighting switch mounted on the instrument panel, also a knob for operating the carburettor choke slide and "tickler" to assist in starting the engine from cold. Standard equipment consists of a driver's saddle, a pillion seat, safety hook for handbag, spare wheel and luggage carrier, and a tool kit stowed in a cylindrical tool box accessible by removing the left-hand side panel.

The frame or chassis comprises a central tubular member which forms the backbone of the scooter. The front forks are mounted in adjustable ball bearings in the steering head on the frame and carry two pivoted links at the lower end to mount the front wheel, each link engages with a compression spring anchored in each fork to provide a sprung suspension. The engine is pivotally mounted to the frame with a single bolt to the front lower frame and forms, in effect, the bottom link of the rear frame section —*see* Fig. 2. Various lugs and brackets bolted to the frame then carry the bolted-on body units which comprise the floorboard and legshield, footrests, centre section fairing over the fuel tank, rear body centre section panel, etc. Detachable side panels complete the fairing-in on the final assembly.

The engine unit comprises a complete, integral group consisting of a near-vertically-mounted single cylinder engine driving a crankshaft running at right angles to the fore-and-aft axis of the scooter and mounting the flywheel dynamo on the left-hand side; a three-speed gearbox bolting directly to the rear face of the crankcase with the primary drive from the engine transmitted to the gearbox via a multiplate clutch; a torque shaft drive from the gearbox running inside the extension of the casing to a secondary gearbox at the rear end, which is bolted to the engine and gearbox unit. The rear hub is also flexibly driven, the transmission being mounted on a swinging arm pivoted on the intermediate gearbox (Fig. 3). Springing is provided by a pair of helical compression springs enclosed in telescopic casings, whilst a shock absorber mounted between the swinging arm and the frame provides damping to promote a more comfortable ride.

Fig. 2. The Prima D in Cut-away Detail, Showing the Method of Rear Suspension

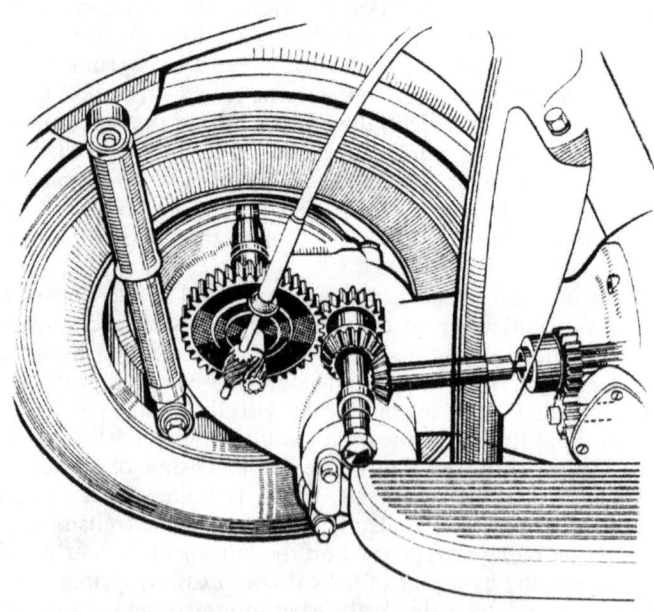

Fig. 3. Prima D Final Drive Details, the Rear Hub Being Flexibly Driven

The handlebars comprise a rigid U-section pressing in steel attached to the top of the forks. The open side of the U-section faces downwards so that all cables can be carried through it out of sight (Fig. 4). A rotatable twist-grip is mounted on the right-hand handlebar connected by cable to the carburettor to provide a throttle control. A similar twist-grip on the left-hand handlebar is connected by cable to the gearbox and actuates the gear-change mechanism. A hand lever on the left-hand side immediately

FIG. 4. PRIMA D HANDLEBARS AND INSTRUMENT PANEL
Also seen in this photo are clamp blocks for a fitted windshield (non standard), left-hand twist grip is gear-change control, right-hand twist-grip the throttle.

in front of the twist-grip operates the clutch, via a cable, and a similar lever on the right-hand side the front brake, again by cable. The rear brake is operated by a foot pedal protruding from the right-hand floorboard. Both brakes are of the internal expanding type, the rear brake being rod-operated.

The Prima V and III follow a similar configuration but with an entirely different engine and transmission layout. The engine is laid sideways with the cylinder pointing to the right-hand side and the flywheel dynamo facing forwards. The crankshaft drive is transmitted via a single dry plate clutch into the four-speed gearbox mounted as a unit integral with the engine. In place of the torque shaft on the Prima D the secondary drive is transmitted direct to the rear wheel via spiral bevel gears (Fig. 5). Gear change is by means of a double-armed rocking lever the ends of which project through the left-hand foot rest in the form of two pedals.

The engine unit is pivotally mounted on two bearings at the rear part of the frame, locating the power unit in the centre of the scooter and providing a desirable weight distribution and low centre of gravity. The method of mounting also provides remarkably good suspension for the rear wheel, in conjunction with a helical compression spring and telescopic hydraulic shock absorber attaching between the rear casing and the frame.

The front forks are of different pattern again, comprising swinging arm suspension of the front wheel in conjunction with a helical compression

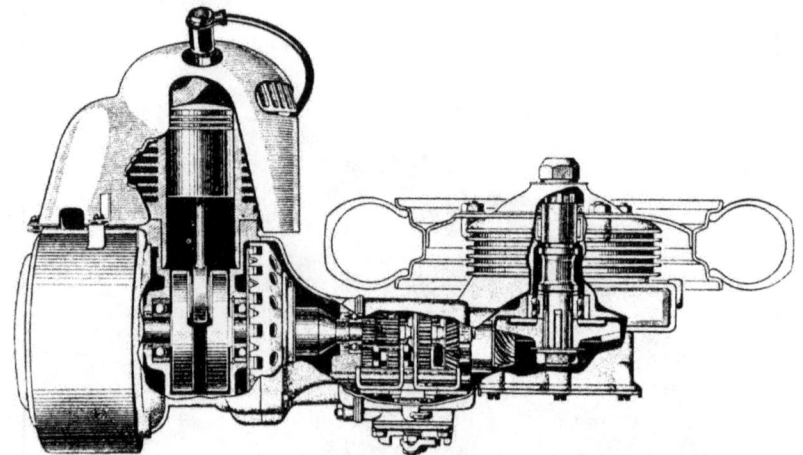

Fig. 5. Details of the Prima V Engine, Clutch, Gearbox and Final Drive are Shown in this Cut-away View

The whole is assembled as an integral unit.

spring and telescopic shock absorber on the left-hand side. Front mudguard, front cowling, instrument panel and headlamp cowling are separate fairings attached to the assembly. The legshield and forward floorboards are an integral cowling, with separate right- and left-hand footrest extensions. The rear mudguard attached to the frame and body fairing is completed with two detachable side panels which also encircle the tank.

Standard features include Dynastart self-starter, battery, headlamp, fog lamp, parking lights and electric horn. Instruments comprise illuminated speedometer, fuel-level warning light, dynamo charging light, combined starting and lighting switch, lighting switch for fog lamp, dip switch, electric horn button and "flasher" light control—all mounted on the instrument panel. In addition, there is a starter knob which acts on the carburettor choke flap to provide a richer mixture for starting in cold weather—but rather different in operation from that on the Prima D— see Chapter III.

Handlebar controls retain the same positions for the throttle twist-grip (right-hand side), front brake lever (right-hand side) and for the clutch lever (left-hand side) (Fig. 6). The handlebar switch group on the left-hand side comprises a dip switch on top (coloured blue), a headlight flasher switch (coloured red) facing to the rear; and on the bottom the horn button (coloured green). The left-hand handlebar grip is, of course, fixed, since gear changing is done via the foot pedals. The rear brake is operated by

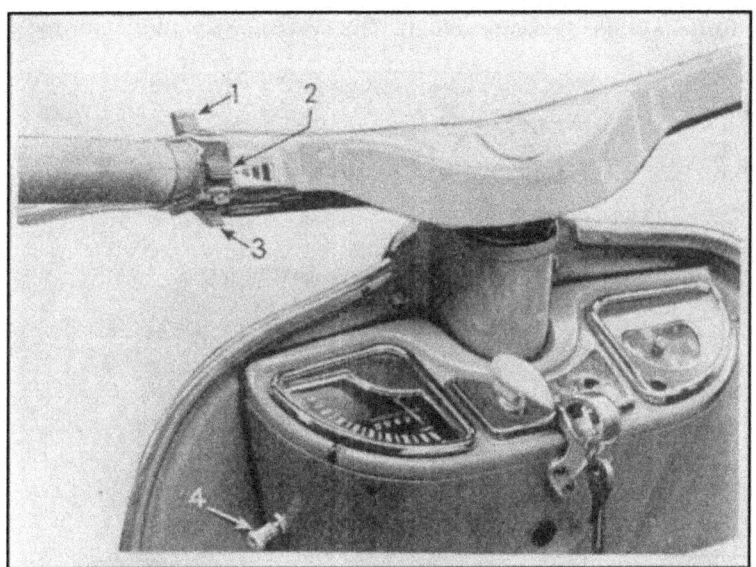

FIG. 6. PRIMA V HANDLEBARS COMPRISE A FIXED LEFT-HAND GRIP

Switch group consists of (1) dip switch; (2) headlight flasher; (3) horn button. Instrument panel also differs. Fog lamp switch (4) is mounted on left-hand side of instrument housing.

a foot pedal on the right-hand side, which protrudes through the floorboard, and is again rod operated.

On the Prima III KL the handlebar group remains basically the same but the instrument panel is not present and a single instrument is mounted on the left-hand cowling with the choke knob immediately in front of it, (*see* Fig. 7). The left-hand handlebar switch group comprises a dip switch (top) and a horn button (rear). The ignition key fits into a socket on top of the headlamp cowling whilst a steering lock is mounted on the down-tube fairing.

Rear brake and gear change are operated by foot pedals, as on the Prima V.

Light Switches. The removable ignition key also acts as a light switch for night driving, or when parking at night. The action is the same on all models—the act of inserting the key switches on the ignition. Depressing the key to its fullest extent operates the starter on the Prima D and Prima V.

With the key in the central position the lights are switched off (although of course, insertion of the key completes the ignition circuit). On the Prima D and V, turning the key to the first "stop" position to the right switches on the parking and tail lights. On the Prima III KL turning the key to the *left* has the same action. The key can be withdrawn from this

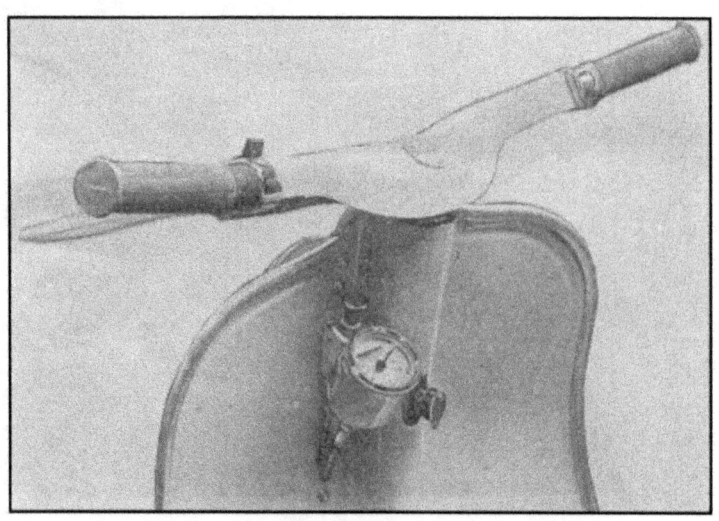

FIG. 7. PRIMA III KL HAS NO INSTRUMENT PANEL

A single instrument (speedometer and mileage recorder) is mounted with the choke knob immediately in front of it. Centre fitting is a handlebar lock. No flasher switch on handlebars; the horn button takes its place.

position (all models), thus leaving the lights on and ignition off. The twin-filament headlamp (and tail lamp) are switched on by turning the key to the second "stop" position to the right (Prima D and V), or fully to the *right* (Prima III KL).

The position of the headlamp beam—full or dipped—then depends on whether or not the dip switch on the handlebars is operated. The dip switch is the *underside* switch on the left-hand handlebar on the Prima D (which may operate either way, depending on the original connexions) and the top switch on the handlebar group on the Prima V and III (*see* Figs. 6 and 7). The Prima V also has a separate fog lamp operated by a switch on the left-hand side of the instrument panel housing (*see* Fig. 6). Pulling this switch out brings the fog lamp into circuit; pushing the switch in switches it off.

Gear Changing—Prima D. The three gear shift positions 1, 2 and 3, together with neutral "0" are marked on the left-hand twist-grip housing (*see* Fig. 8). A mark on the moving part attached to the twist-grip indicates which gear is engaged. This control should never be operated without pulling in the clutch lever even when the engine is not running as this can put unnecessary strain on the cables. The gear change should always be left in neutral when the scooter is not in use. If not, it can be put into neutral by pulling in the clutch lever, turning the twist-grip to "0" and rocking the scooter backwards and forwards, if necessary, to release the

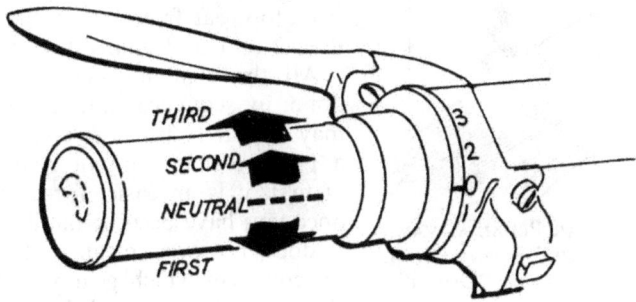

Fig. 8. Gear Change is Manually Operated on the Prima D through the Left-hand Twist-grip

gears. Change positions when driving, using the clutch each time, are then—

1st gear—rotating the twist-grip to position "1,"
2nd gear—rotating the twist-grip through "0" to position "2,"
3rd gear—rotating the twist-grip one more step to position "3."

The absolute beginner may need a little practice to "feel" the correct engagement of each gear—he may, for instance, tend to change from 1st to 3rd, passing right through 2nd gear position for a start—but very little practice should be needed to establish the correct change positions when it will become a more or less automatic reaction.

Changing down follows the opposite sequence. *Any* gear can, in fact, be selected once the clutch is pulled in, but in any of the driving gears 1, 2 or 3, it may be necessary to adjust engine speed before letting out the clutch again—*see* later.

Gear Changing—Prima V and III. The gearbox on the Prima V and III is operated on a sequence principle, using the two foot pedals on the left-hand running board (*see* Fig. 9). The *rear* pedal operates for changing *up* and the *front* pedal for changing *down*. The clutch must, of course, be pulled in when making a gear change.

Starting from neutral, pressing down with the foot on the rear lever automatically selects 1st gear, i.e. moves the gearbox position from 0 to 1. For the next change up, declutch and press down on the rear pedal again to shift from 1 to 2, and so on for 2 to 3 and finally 3 to 4. Further pressure on the rear gear-change pedal will have no effect.

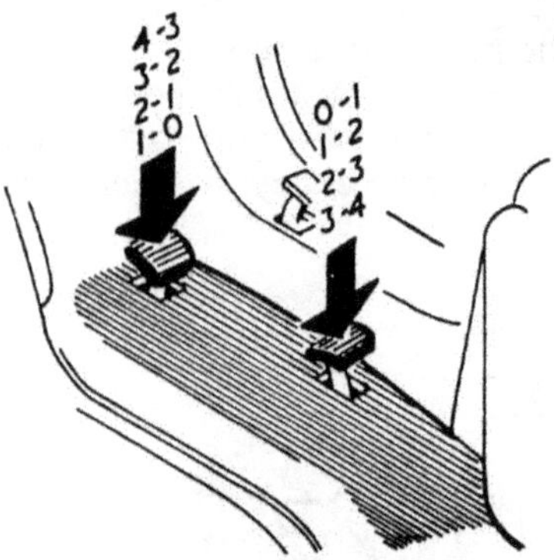

To change down the front pedal is depressed (again declutching each time). Each down stroke on this pedal changes down *one* gear—i.e. starting from top gear from 4 to 3, then 3 to 2, then 2 to 1 and finally 1 to 0.

All the changing—up or down—is done in sequence and although this may appear to be more confusing than a positive indication of gear position at first, it is an easier form of control once you have become familiar with it. It does, however, mean that you have to remember which gear you are in to change back to neutral, but the operation soon becomes automatic. Neutral position is always indicated, in any case, on either pedal by the fact that no further movement of the pedal is possible.

FIG. 9. REAR PEDAL ALWAYS CHANGES "UP," FRONT PEDAL ALWAYS CHANGES "DOWN"

Purpose and Use of the Gearbox. The reason for having a gearbox on all road vehicles is clear to the mechanically-minded, but confusing to many who are not familiar with the operation of scooters, motor-cycles or cars. The following simple explanation is appended to show why a gearbox is necessary and how it is used. Once the principle involved is clearly understood driving technique can only improve as a consequence and the mystery of a gearbox is no more. On the contrary, it is appreciated for what it really is—a very useful part of the machine which makes it capable of operating under all sorts of driving conditions.

For a start we have just the engine, the speed of which is controlled by the throttle twist-grip. The engine develops a turning force or *torque* applied to its crankshaft which tends to decrease as the engine speed increases. The *power* developed by the engine, however, is the product of *torque* and *speed* or r.p.m. Thus if we plot these two factors on a simple graph as shown in Fig. 10 (*left*) we find maximum power developed at a certain engine r.p.m. figure. This is termed the "peak" r.p.m. of the engine. If we push the speed up still further, although the engine may be running faster it is developing *less* driving power and so its performance is falling off.

If now we ally this to a complete drive where the engine is powering a

BASIC DESIGN AND LAYOUT 15

roadwheel we cannot drive the wheel direct all the time but must gear down the crankshaft speed in order to get a satisfactory intermediate performance. Peak engine speed of the NSU engine, for example, is 5,100 r.p.m. If this drove the 3·50 wheel direct, without slip, this would be equivalent to a road speed of some 200 m.p.h.! The scooter would never reach this speed because its resistance to motion would increase rapidly with speed—approximately as the square of the speed—and the power absorbed at this theoretical maximum speed would be greater than the engine can give (i.e. greater than the maximum horse-power of the engine).

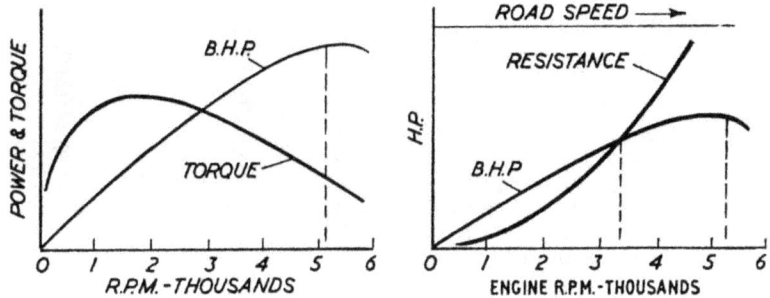

Fig. 10. Typical Curve of Horse-power and Torque Developed Against Engine r.p.m. (*left*) and Road Resistance against Speed (*right*)

The two curves would cross at some lower speed—see Fig. 10 (*right*)—which would be the absolute maximum speed with direct drive.

Note now that this corresponds to an engine speed *lower* than the r.p.m. at which the engine develops maximum power. In other words, with such a set-up the maximum power of the engine could never be realized. Hence an overall gear ratio has to be worked out for the design which allows the maximum speed achieved to *correspond* to peak engine speed and power. That is then an excellent arrangement for top gear.

Now that this is settled, however, there remains the problem of what happens at lower speeds, for the scooter can never be driven continuously at top speed. With a suitable overall gear ratio for a maximum speed, driving at any other speed means, simply, that only a proportion of the power of the engine can be used, and the lower the speed the lower the power available from the engine for driving (*see* Fig. 11 (*left*)). The result would be very poor acceleration and lack of pulling power—and complete inability to climb hills, or possibly even to start away from a standstill.

Hence the necessity of having available a number of other *different* gear ratios, which can be selected at will. Each will have its own maximum engine r.p.m. and engine power at a certain speed. Remembering that the engine peak speed is 5,000 r.p.m. it is a matter of simple mathematics to arrive at top speeds in different overall gear ratios so that with four different gear ratios available we have a family of curves, as in Fig. 11 (*right*), each representing a speed range associated with a particular gear and optimum performance from the engine within each range. In first gear there is plenty of power available at quite low speeds—compared with the power which would be available at the same engine speed in any other

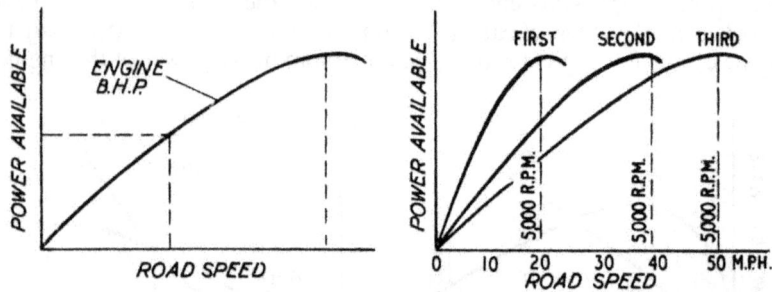

FIG. 11. WITHOUT GEARING, (*left*) ROAD SPEED ACHIEVED WOULD BE LIMITED TO MUCH LESS THAN FULL PERFORMANCE OF THE ENGINE, AVAILABLE OVER A WIDE SPEED RANGE (*right*) WITH GEARS

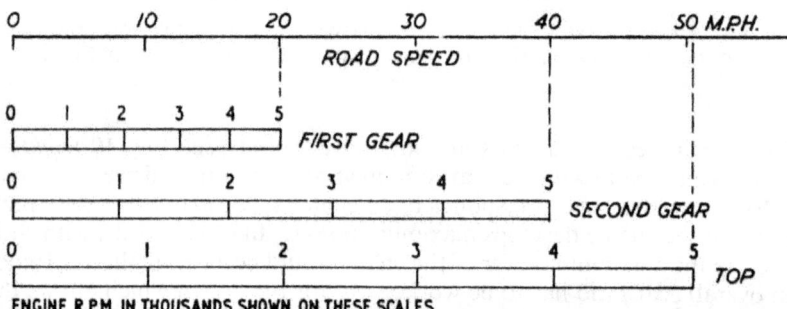

FIG. 12. ROAD SPEED AGAINST ENGINE R.P.M. SIMPLY PLOTTED FOR DIFFERENT GEARS

These apply to approximate performance of the Prima D with three-speed gearbox.

gear, for instance—but a limit to top speed and similarly in the other intermediate gears. All the respective curves overlap to a certain extent to give a smooth transition changing from one gear to another.

Now let us translate this in terms of engine speeds and road speeds in the various gears (Fig. 12). This diagram should now be more or less self-explanatory, the important point to appreciate being that accelerating up to a speed in a lower gear where a change "up" is called for the engine speed realized in the lower gear is very much higher than the engine speed in the higher gear for the same road speed. In other words, during the act of changing gear the *engine* must also be throttled down to adjust to the new gear ratio. Similarly, in changing *down*, the engine must be speeded *up* to engage smoothly at the same road speed. Hence the use of the throttle control when gear changing, as described in the next chapter.

APPROXIMATE MAXIMUM SPEEDS IN GEARS

GEAR	PRIMA D	PRIMA V	PRIMA III KL
1st	18 m.p.h.	15 m.p.h.	15 m.p.h.
2nd	30 m.p.h.	22 m.p.h.	24 m.p.h.
3rd	50 m.p.h.	35 m.p.h.	32 m.p.h.
4th	—	55 m.p.h.	50 m.p.h.

APPROXIMATE "CHANGE" SPEEDS
CHANGING UP

GEAR CHANGE	PRIMA D	PRIMA V	PRIMA III KL
1st to 2nd	10–15 m.p.h.	8–12 m.p.h.	8–10 m.p.h.
2nd to 3rd	25–28 m.p.h.	15–18 m.p.h.	18–22 m.p.h.
3rd to 4th	—	25–30 m.p.h.	25–28 m.p.h.

CHANGING DOWN[1]

GEAR CHANGE	PRIMA D	PRIMA V	PRIMA III KL
4th to 3rd	—	30–25 m.p.h.	30–25 m.p.h.
3rd to 2nd	20 m.p.h.	25–20 m.p.h.	20 m.p.h.
2nd to 1st	Under 10 m.p.h.	Under 6–8 m.p.h.	Under 6–8 m.p.h.

[1] Speed for changing down does, of course, depend on driving conditions. An early change-down is advisable under heavy load, e.g. when climbing a steep or long hill, to avoid loss of engine speed. The higher the load, too, the higher the speed at which the engine will tend to "snatch" when driving in top gear.

CHAPTER III

OPERATION AND HANDLING

THE disposition of the various controls, etc., on the various models has already been described in Chapter II. The new owner can familiarize himself (or herself) by sitting astride the machine and maintaining balance with one foot on the ground and trying them out without the engine running. The gear-change control (twist-grip on the Prima D, foot-change pedals on the Prima V and III) should *not* be operated in such a preliminary try-out, however. The new owner should also check how the side panels are removed to gain access to the engine unit, how to remove the batteries, the setting of the prop stand, etc.

The prop stand is fitted on the left-hand side of the machine and is hinged to pull down and form a rigid strut, so that the scooter can be left resting on it in a near upright position for parking. The second stand located approximately in the centre (on the Prima D—or on the right-hand side, Prima V and III) is a *jacking* stand, used only to support the scooter when changing a wheel or to take the weight of the machine off the tyres should the scooter be laid up for a long period. The Prima III KL has a left-hand prop stand only. One should never try to sit on the saddle when the scooter is supported on either of these stands. The prop stand provides adequate support for the scooter only on substantially level, hard surfaces. It will not necessarily be effective on a soft surface where it may sink in.

The petrol tank filler is located between the driver's and pillion saddles—to the right in the case of the Prima D and covered by a hinged flap; central in the case of the Prima V and III with the filler cap protruding above the panelling. Fuel capacity of the tank is 21 pints and 2·9 gallons, respectively.

The level of the petrol in the tank can be established by using a length of clean wooden stick as a dipstick, visually by looking in the tank, or by rocking the machine gently from side to side to estimate the approximate contents. A fuel-warning light on the instrument panel shows as a red light when the tank is running low with the ignition switched on. When the fuel-warning lamp first starts to glow there are only $3\frac{1}{4}$ pints of fuel remaining in the tank, $2\frac{1}{4}$ pints in the case of the Prima D and $3\frac{3}{4}$ pints in the case of the Prima V—sufficient in actual fact for a further 30–40 miles driving under average conditions. There is no fuel-warning lamp on the III KL but a "reserve" supply is governed by the fuel tap position.

The tank is fitted with a fuel tap (*see* Fig. 13) which is operated by insertion of the ignition key, as shown. When the key is in the horizontal position the fuel tap is closed and no fuel can drain from the tank into the carburettor. With the key in the vertical position the tap is open for normal running. On the Prima III KL the ignition switch is again used to operate the tap, but this time it has three positions. "Off" and "on" correspond to the positions just described, but turning the tap to the *right* (viewed from the front) switches on the reserve supply of fuel in the tank. This is in lieu of the warning light fitted to the other models and provides

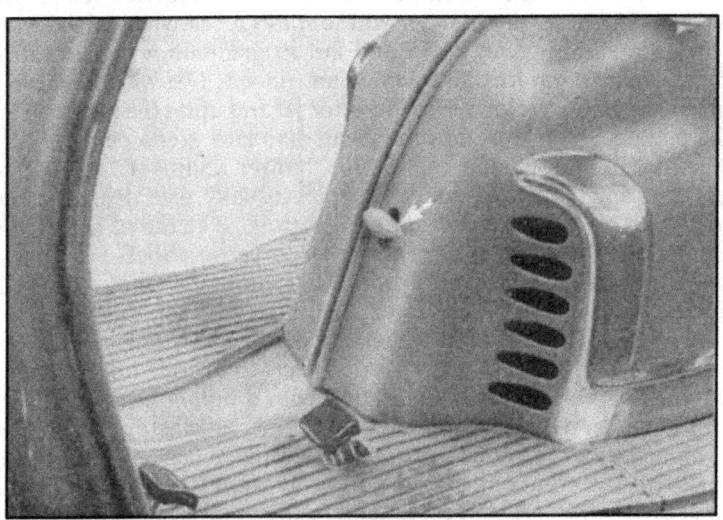

FIG. 13. FUEL TAP (ARROWED) IS OPERATED BY THE IGNITION KEY ON ALL MODELS

Has two positions on Prima V, but also a "reserve" switching position on the Prima III KL.

a similar safety measure—always assuming that the tap is used properly and not switched to "reserve" position in the first case instead of normal "on."

General practice is to close the tap after a run or when parking for any time to avoid any chance of the engine becoming "flooded," and to open again when restarting. It is not necessary to close the tap when stopping for just a short period. At the end of a day's run, however, it is good practice to stop the engine by closing the tap and letting the engine run dry, rather than simply to switch off the ignition. This will prevent any possibility of the carburettor jet oiling up, which could make for difficult starting next time.

Standard grade petrol is the fuel for the Prima engine but all two-stroke engines of this type are designed without any separate lubrication system so the necessary lubricating oil is mixed with the petrol. *It is imperative* that the recommended petrol-oil mixture be used in he tank all the time (*see* Chapter IV) and never petrol alone as if there is no oil in the mixture the piston will quickly "seize" in the cylinder and result in expensive damage.

It is also extremely important that the correct *grade* of oil be used in the petrol-oil mixture. For all Prima engines this is SAE 40 grade. The SAE number of an oil is a measure of its viscosity or thickness. The higher the SAE number the thicker or more viscous the oil, and vice versa. An oil with a low SAE viscosity number will thin too much when mixed with the petrol and possibly break down and fail to maintain a film of lubricant over the rubbing surfaces. Too thick an oil—i.e. one with a higher SAE number—will tend to clog the carburettor jet and upset the mixture supply.

There is no point in using other than standard grade petrol, however. Higher octane petrols, and those with "power additives" are not really suited to simple two-stroke engines which usually give their best overall performance on the cheaper "straight" petrols. The use of heavily doped fuels may even be harmful or detrimental to performance.

Recommended petrol-oil proportions fall within the range 20:1 to 24:1, equivalent to 1 pint of oil per 2½ or 3 gallons of petrol, respectively. The slightly oilier mixture is used when running-in a new engine (e.g. for the first 500 miles or so), or when the scooter has to operate under heavy load conditions, such as continual operation with a pillion passenger, running in very hilly country, etc. The 24:1 mixture is satisfactory for all general running under normal conditions, once the engine has been run in. *There is no economy at all* in reducing the oil proportion still further as although the fuel cost will be less (oil costing more than petrol) wear and deterioration of the engine will be higher so that maintenance costs will rise. If the proportion of oil is reduced beyond the recommended limits, too, there is every chance that lubrication will be insufficient, rapidly leading to complete breakdown of the engine.

Increasing the oil ratio—i.e. using more oil than that recommended will *not* provide more or better lubrication. The surplus oil will simply be burnt, leading to rapid sooting up of the inside of the engine and silencer, and excess oil will also tend to collect on the spark plug, and to foul it.

When filling the tank the fuel tap should always be turned to the "off" position and the petrol run in first. Oil added to the top of the petrol then disperses through it with less risk of unmixed oil collecting at the bottom of the tank and being drawn, undiluted, into the carburettor when the tap is opened again. Usually completely satisfactory dispersion of the oil through the petrol can be obtained by shaking the scooter from side to side a few times after filling. Two-stroke self-mixing oils are formulated for rapid dispersion in petrol and as dispensed at local garages normally give complete mixing without any need for subsequent shaking.

It is also considered good practice—usually not necessary, but a good precaution—to agitate the mixture in the tank before starting if the scooter has been standing unused for a few days. This would be done before opening the fuel tap as a preliminary measure.

A point often overlooked, but one of considerable importance, is to ensure always that only clean fuel is allowed to enter the tank. Fuel should never be dispensed through a dirty funnel. Any grime around the

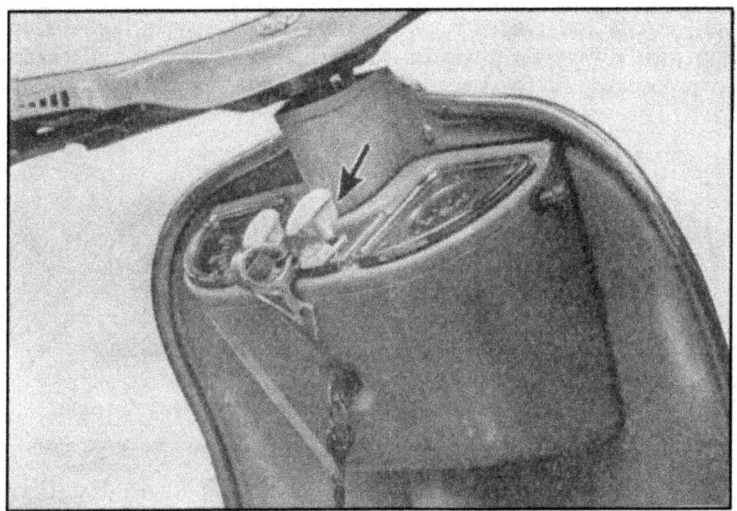

FIG. 14. KEY (ARROWED) IS INSERTED TO COMPLETE IGNITION CIRCUIT. DEPRESS TO OPERATE STARTER, OR TURN TO SWITCH ON LIGHTS

edges of cans, or the tank filler, should be wiped off with a clean cloth so that no foreign particles are carried down into the tank. Such particles will not reach the engine since they will be trapped in the filter gauze in the tap, or in the main filter, but by partially clogging the filter they will upset the mixture and thus interfere with the running of the engine.

STARTING THE ENGINE

Starting procedure with all self-starter models is—
1. Open the fuel tap.
2. Make sure that the gearbox is in neutral.
3. Operate the choke knob as described below.
4. Check that the throttle twist-grip is closed.
5. Insert the ignition key in the combined starting and lighting switch, when the red ignition light will glow indicating that the batteries are switched on and supplying current. Then *depress* the ignition key firmly into the ignition lock to operate the starter.

The engine should start more or less immediately. If it does not start within three of four seconds, release the ignition key *otherwise you will run the battery right down*. Wait for a while to give the battery time to recover, say a matter of ten seconds in warm weather, longer in cold weather, and then depress the ignition key again. If the engine fails to start after three or four such attempts something is wrong and the fault must be found and remedied. Prolonged use of the starter with no effect will flatten the batteries completely.

It must be appreciated that the size of battery carried by the Prima is relatively small and the current demand from a starter high. Current demand will be highest in winter, when the engine is stiff and harder to turn over because of the thickening of the oil. The immediate current

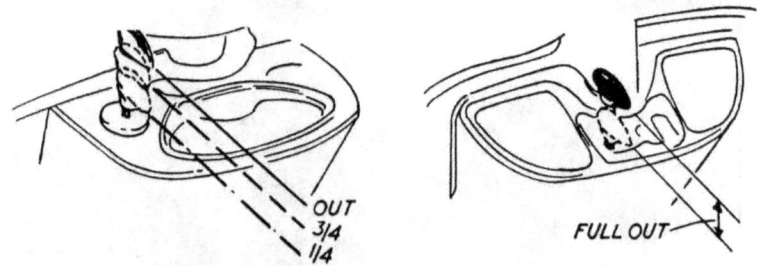

FIG. 15. CHOKE CONTROL PRIMA D (*left*) AND PRIMA V (*right*)

On the Prima III KL the choke knob is immediately in front of the speedometer (*see* Fig. 7).

drain may approach a hundred amps and the battery cannot cope with such a demand continuously *for more than a few seconds*. A brief rest and it will recover again, but this process cannot be continued indefinitely. So, always be as easy as possible on the battery. It helps, too, in very cold weather if the scooter can be kept in a sheltered or warmer place rather than being left outside to "soak" in the cold all night.

The Choke Control. The choke control on all Prima models is unusual in operation. It is operated by the choke knob on the left-hand side of the instrument panel (*see* Fig. 15). On the Prima D, pulling this knob out to its fullest extent closes a choke slide in the main body of the air inlet silencer and also depresses a tickler on the carburettor to depress the float and allow fuel to flood into the float chamber. With the choke knob pulled three-quarters out (i.e. pushed in one-quarter from the full out position) the tickler is released but the choke slide remains fully closed. Further closing of the choke knob (i.e. pushing it down into the instrument panel) then progressively opens the choke slide. With the choke knob one-quarter out the choke slide is half open. With the choke knob pushed right in, the choke slide is fully open.

Pulling the choke knob right out, therefore, operates the tickler to flood the carburettor. This action is normally only required to "prime" the carburettor after the scooter has been left standing for a long period, or for

OPERATION AND HANDLING

starting in very cold weather. It should not be necessary to hold the choke knob in the fully open position for more than a few seconds to ensure adequate filling of the carburettor. Leaving it open too long will result in flooding and a wet engine which will prove difficult to start.

The exact procedure to be followed for best starting is a technique best established on a trial-and-error basis on the lines of the following recommendations, for starting from cold.

In very cold weather—

   (a) pull choke knob right out and hold for 5–10 seconds;
   (b) close choke knob to three-quarter-open position;
   (c) operate starter to get engine running;
   (d) close choke knob down to quarter-open position, then fully close as soon as the engine will run steadily.

In average weather—

as above, but restrict the time with choke knob fully out to 5 seconds.

In warm weather—

pull choke knob right out and immediately return to three-quarter-open position. Then operate starter and close choke as soon as the engine is running—dwelling in an intermediate choke position, as necessary, to keep the engine running without misfiring or "spitting."

In all cases, if the engine starts and then stops again when the choke knob is pushed in, open the choke knob to the three-quarter-open position and leave there until the engine has warmed up and is running smoothly. The engine should always be warmed up to the point where it is running smoothly with the choke knob *fully pushed down* before starting off, otherwise you may drive away and continue to drive with the choke open without realizing it. This will result in the engine's running on a very rich mixture, giving lack of pulling power.

When the engine is warm, or in hot weather after the initial morning start, restarting can usually be accomplished without using the choke control at all. Use the choke as necessary if (1) the engine fails to fire, indicating lack of fuel, or (2) the engine starts and then stops again almost immediately.

With the Prima V and III the choke knob acts on the carburettor in a slightly different way. Pulling the knob right out raises a small plunger in a separate chamber on the carburettor. There is no separate choke flap. Operation of the choke knob by pulling it in and out literally pumps fuel into the carburettor for priming—equivalent to the tickler action on the Prima D carburettor. Holding the choke knob out in a stationary position gives a choke effect on the fuel supply to the engine by allowing passage of extra fuel from this separate chamber (refer to Fig. 15).

Action required is, therefore, use the choke knob as a pump to prime in very cold conditions and the choke knob fully out for normal "choke" effect. In warm weather—or with a warm engine—starting should be achieved without having to touch the choke knob. In average conditions, starting from cold, pulling the choke knob out to its fully open position should provide all the necessary choke action required. The choke knob is left out in this position until the engine is running freely.

The most common cause of starting trouble is *too much fuel* being drawn into the engine—e.g. through excessive use of the tickler (Prima D) or pumping the choke knob (Prima V and III). This results in the sparking plug electrode's becoming wet when it will not produce the required spark to fire the mixture. In bad cases of flooding the excess of petrol will be apparent by its smell and the fact that it is running down the sides of the carburettor.

The only satisfactory remedy in this case is to close the fuel tap, remove the spark plug and dry it thoroughly (e.g. by blowing on it) or, preferably, to replace it with a clean, dry plug. Engaging second gear and pushing the scooter along or running on the starter with the spark plug removed to pump excess mixture out through the spark plug hole may also help to clear the cylinder of excess fuel. Replace the plug and start again without using the choke until the engine fires. Then, if necessary, you can open up the choke as required to promote smooth running until the engine has properly warmed up.

If the flooding is less drastic it can often be cleared by closing the choke knob, opening the throttle wide and then operating the starter in bursts until the engine fires. It is worth repeating that *flooding is the chief cause of starting difficulty*, and over-generous use of the choke control the cause.

If the starter battery has been run down and will not turn the starter, the engine can be started by engaging second gear and then pushing the scooter along, running with it until firing commences. Immediately disengage the clutch and change to neutral. Note, however, that if the batteries have been removed, e.g. for recharging, the ignition circuit is broken and so to get a spark for a push-start (and for the engine to continue running), the charging lead (coloured red) from the cut-out must be connected to the lead attached to the positive battery lead and taped to protect it against shorting out (*see* Fig. 66). As a general rule it can be said that push-starting is *not* recommended with the Prima D as it can cause damage to the transmission. It can, however, be employed with the other models as an emergency method.

Kick-start Prima III KL. Starting procedure is virtually identical for the Prima III K and III KL except that the kick-starter pedal (Fig. 16) must be depressed smartly with the right foot to spin the engine over, after first inserting the ignition key. Choke operation is the same as on the Prima V. The necessary foot action for kick-starting readily becomes familiar with a little practice and should present no difficulties to any individual although the pedal position may be found awkward at first. If the settings are correct—i.e. proper action with the choke knob and throttle closed or very nearly closed—starting should be accomplished in not more than two or three kick strokes. If it does not start within half a dozen kicks then the cause should be investigated as further kicking over will probably only make matters worse—e.g. result in flooding.

Kick-starter motion required is a smooth, powerful down stroke. Jabbing at the starter pedal with the foot will be ineffective as well as put

FIG. 16. KICK-STARTER PEDAL (ARROWED) ON PRIMA III KL HAS A TYPICAL "CONTINENTAL" ACTION, DIFFICULT TO MASTER AT FIRST
Ignition switch is on top of the headlamp.

unnecessary strain on the gear teeth. The same consideration applies to models fitted with self-starters. Jabbing at the starter control is a fault which must be avoided as it may result in stripped gears.

If the battery is removed from the Prima III KL the engine can be operated normally by disconnecting the white/black lead at the snap connector leading to the contact-breaker (see Fig. 67). In this case the ignition switch is rendered ineffective and no key is required for switching on the ignition since this is permanently in closed circuit—a useful tip to remember if the ignition key is lost!

DRIVING TECHNIQUE

Once the engine is running smoothly, you can, sitting astride the machine, engage first gear by pulling in the clutch lever and selecting first gear, as described in Chapter II (with the twist-grip in the case of the Prima D and rearward foot change pedal in the case of the Prima V and III). The throttle should then be opened to about one-third with a slow movement and *simultaneously* the clutch lever released *slowly and evenly* so that the drive picks up smoothly. The scooter will then pull away without jerking.

The object of opening the throttle *simultaneously* with releasing the clutch is to allow the engine to develop more power to take up the extra load that is being put upon it to drive the scooter forward. The object of releasing the clutch *slowly* is to allow the drive connexion between the engine and the back wheel (via the gearbox and transmission) to slip at first and then *progressively* take up the load so that the pull away is smooth and not jerky. If the scooter jerks forward suddenly and the engine stops, the load has been applied too abruptly—usually because the clutch has been let out too quickly. This can also happen if the throttle is not open enough and the load applied by releasing the clutch is too much for the engine. In the former case the jerk forward will be very abrupt. In the latter case, if the clutch has been let out very slowly, the engine will start to labour and the final jerk as it stops will be slight.

Another thing that can happen is for the "take off" to be accomplished with a violent jerk, but the engine continues running and the scooter continues to motor along. This is caused by the throttle being opened *too much*, and possibly also aggravated by letting the clutch out a little too rapidly.

It is important that a newcomer to scooter driving appreciates these points as by understanding what has caused the trouble he can apply the appropriate remedy and quickly master his machine with a minimum of practice. Beginners, too, should always start with a straight and clear run in front of them. That curved drive may seem a less conspicuous place to start, but it is far more difficult to negotiate on an initial run than a straight road.

Another tip for the absolute beginner—particularly those who are not mechanically-minded—is that whatever the state of panic which may develop when they find themselves moving off and in sole charge of a motor vehicle for the first time, pulling both handlebar levers will bring them to a stop! The one will disengage the engine from driving, and the other will apply the front brake. All they then have to remember is to close the throttle and change back to neutral gear position before releasing the clutch lever.

The motor-scooter is stable at a very low forward speed, so once moving there is no need to trail a tentative foot—or both feet—over the side. All the necessary control can be achieved via the steering and the scooter is possibly easier, in this respect, to control than a pedal bicycle. The speed of motion is, of course, directly controlled by the position of the throttle twist-grip.

Driving in first gear a maximum speed of about 12 m.p.h. can be reached, at which road speed the engine is operating at maximum r.p.m. At about 12 m.p.h., therefore, it becomes necessary to change up into a higher gear so that the ratio between the *engine speed* and *road speed* is reduced, and similarly through the range of the gearbox.

This is done by simultaneously closing the throttle and pulling in the clutch lever. The latter disengages the engine drive from the gearbox, closing the throttle prevents the engine speeding up as the load is removed. Now select second gear position and let out the clutch evenly again, at the same time opening the throttle slowly. The process is repeated at a higher speed for changing up into the next gear (top in the case of the Prima D and third in the case of the Prima V and III); and once more to get into top gear on the Prima V and III. Recommended speeds at which changing should be made, and also an explanation of the purpose of the gearbox, have already been given in Chapter II.

Faults which develop when changing up should be self-apparent. If the engine races as you start to change, the throttle has not been closed simultaneously with operating the clutch. A pronounced braking effect before you have disengaged the clutch means that the throttle has been closed too quickly. A "snatch" or jerk as the clutch is released after changing gear means that the throttle should have been opened up a little as the clutch was let out to compensate for the actual road speed at the time (in this case rather higher than the recommended figure).

The process of changing up should be accomplished smoothly and reasonably quickly. There is no need to rush the operation, neither should the engine be allowed to "dwell" in the declutched position for an excessive time so that road speed may be lost. The clutch can be let out much more rapidly than when pulling away from a standing start in first gear and co-ordination of control movements is easy to master.

When changing *down* the technique is slightly different. Declutch first so that the engine speed will *increase* as the load comes off the engine and immediately adjust the throttle position to approximate to an engine speed consistent with the road speed at the moment in the lower gear. This sounds highly technical but is something which comes quite readily with practice. It means, simply, allow the engine to speed up when declutched so that when the lower gear is engaged and the clutch released again the drive will pick up without a jerk. Study of the section in Chapter II dealing with the gearbox should make this point about *increasing* engine speed when *changing down* clear. In point of fact the gearbox is designed to compensate for a considerable degree of speed difference so that the gears may be engaged easily, but using the throttle to assist the gearbox is good driving technique and should always be practised.

Changing down is usually necessary when climbing a hill of any appreciable gradient. This allows the engine to work harder, as it were, and develop more power for the climb by running at a faster (engine) speed for the same road speed. Slogging up a gradient in a high gear means that the engine is labouring and loses speed and power, as well as putting extra load on the bearings. The engine itself will show signs of distress by emitting a knocking or rattling sound or the drive will commence to "snatch" or jerk, emphasizing that it is driving through too low a gear ratio! Good driving demands changing down in plenty of time, particularly when approaching a steep hill.

Exactly the same form of snatch or jerky motion in the transmission can be experienced by changing up too quickly, i.e. at too low a road speed. The Prima D, for example, will not pull smoothly in top gear at less than 20 m.p.h. If allowed to slow down to this figure in top gear, or changed up into top gear at a road speed lower than this figure, it will not pull smoothly. In the case of the Prima V and III minimum speed for smooth running in top gear is about 25 m.p.h. and 20 m.p.h., respectively.

Changing down a gear is also a good method of slowing down when approaching a corner or behind a moving obstruction. Changing down to second gear (Prima D) or third gear (Prima V and III) and closing the throttle will cause the engine to act as a brake, at the same time being ready for rapid acceleration again by opening up the throttle when the way is clear. The four-speed gearbox of the Prima V and III offers more flexibility in this respect than the Prima D because of the two intermediate gears available between top and bottom gears.

General Driving Technique. The good driver always uses the gearbox properly, and to full advantage. Frequent changes may be necessary when driving in traffic. On the open roads where a steady speed can be maintained the engine is simply left in top gear, but getting into the habit of continual "top gear" driving is bad where speed variations are concerned. The basic rule is to use the gearbox whenever necessary as a matter of good driving, but not excessively under driving conditions which do not warrant it.

When the scooter has to be brought to a stop at traffic obstacles, etc., the gear position should *always* be shifted to neutral and the engine left to idle with the clutch released.

The practice of slipping the clutch, i.e. holding the clutch fully in to disengage the engine with a gear engaged, when stationary *is to be condemned*. It is very bad driving practice and promotes rapid wear on the clutch plates. Similarly, slipping the clutch to avoid stalling the engine when climbing a hill is equally bad—and equally damaging to the clutch mechanism.

If the engine is left to idle or run slowly with the throttle closed for any length of time there will be a tendency for the oil distribution throughout the engine to be incomplete. In other words, with the engine running very slowly insufficient oil may be splashed over the rubbing surfaces to maintain a satisfactory film of lubricant. In addition, there may be a tendency for the engine to overheat, aggravating this condition.

The solution in such cases is to give a burst of throttle occasionally, just to draw in a large charge of mixture and distribute more oil around the inside of the engine. Normally, of course, one would not leave the engine idling unnecessarily with the scooter stationary, but exactly the same considerations apply when descending a long hill where the throttle may be closed completely so that the engine acts as a brake. This is worse than the "stationary" case since the engine is actually being turned over faster, but with a very minimum of oil supply.

It is, therefore, important when using the engine as a brake on such occasions to pull in the clutch momentarily every few hundred yards (holding the scooter on the brakes) and give a quick burst of throttle.

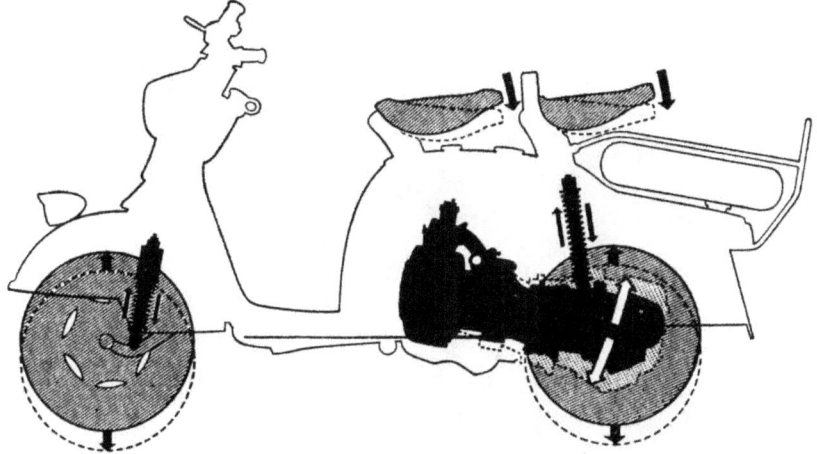

FIG. 17. SUSPENSION AND SPRINGING ON THE PRIMA V

This becomes *more important* the lower the gear selected, simply because the lower the gear the faster the engine will be turning over. It is not generally recommended, therefore, to use the lower gears as a brake when descending hills of any length, except in the case of very steep hills where assistance to the normal brakes is highly desirable. Even then the engine should be given bursts of throttle every hundred yards or so.

For normal braking, most efficient action comes from using both the front and rear brakes together, at the same time closing the throttle. This ensures even wear on brake linings and tyres. Descending hills both brakes can be used together again, or the front and rear brakes used alternately to prevent overheating. The front brake should *not* be used for braking on wet or slippery roads. Under such conditions rely on the rear brake only. However, getting into the habit of using the rear brake only—because it is so convenient and easy to apply—is *bad* driving practice. *Both* brakes should normally be used together, within the limitations just described. Uneven wear on brake linings is a sign that one or other brake is being used excessively.

There is a distinct difference in the behaviour of the three models, due to the different suspension of the front wheels. The best action is on the Prima V where the pivoted links are mounted on the fork and the links are long, with the wheel in front of the pivot point. The Prima III KL has a similar form of front wheel mounting, but with slightly shorter links. The Prima D has short links and the wheel trails the pivot point and so is much more prone to "dipping" when the brakes are applied hard.

Cornering. Cornering is quite straightforward: in fact the small wheel diameter and low centre of gravity make the scooter remarkably safe and

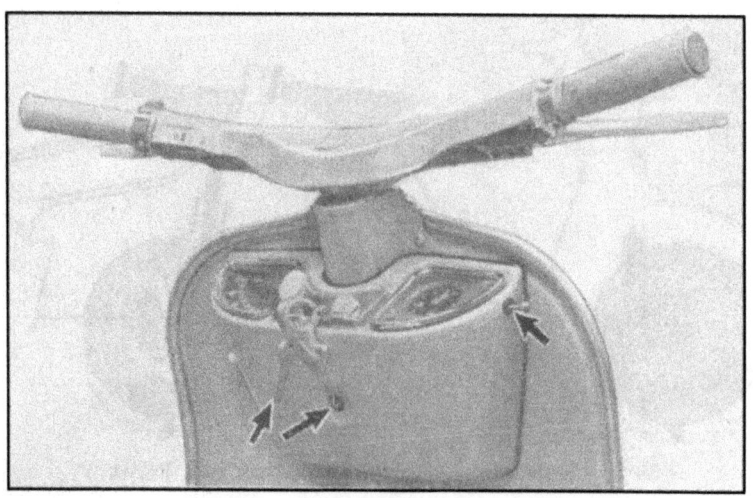

FIG. 18. YALE-TYPE KEY FITS HANDLEBAR LOCK. KNOB ON RIGHT (ARROWED) IS FOR WINDING AND SETTING CLOCK ON INSTRUMENT PANEL

manoeuvrable on good road surfaces. As with all two-wheeled vehicles when cornering there is an outward force generated (centrifugal force) acting through the centre of gravity tending to topple the machine outwards. This is counteracted by leaning inwards into the turn, the rider's sense of balance automatically adjusting the amount of lean in or "bank" to the correct amount. Because of the low centre of gravity the "overturning" moment is also low, but so also is the effective counter-force produced by leaning into the turn. Thus for the same speed, weight and turning circle, a scooter needs just the same *angle* of bank as a motorcycle, although it is inherently more stable.

Stability in fast, steeply banked turns is finally dependent on the adhesion between the tyres and the road surface. In wet weather, and on treacherous surfaces such as wet leaves, adhesion can be poor, so that adopting the necessary angle of bank may produce a condition where one wheel or both wheels start to slip sideways. This immediately increases the angle of bank and things become worse, with the whole machine sliding away from under the rider. This can happen so suddenly that even an experienced rider is taken unawares and cannot take countermeasures in time.

The real answer is to avoid such situations, driving cautiously on wet or slippery roads, going into corners more slowly and taking them more widely so that you are using only the minimum amount of bank necessary. If a slide develops on a slippery surface, never apply brakes to attempt to stop or correct it, as this will only make matters worse. If a slide develops on braking, release the brakes and declutch *immediately*. The correct action in the case of a back wheel slide is to turn *into* the direction in which the wheel is sliding. Correcting a front wheel slide is more difficult for the time available for applying correction may be almost negligible. The correct action is to open the throttle and try to straighten out by accelerating.

Stopping and Parking. At the end of a journey, or when parking, the engine is stopped by closing the throttle and removing the ignition key. The ignition key should always be removed and the cover plate folded down over the switch to protect it against rain, etc. Then use the ignition key to turn the fuel tap to the closed position. The Prima III KL has no protective cover over the ignition swivel socket and it is advisable to cover this if the machine is left out in rain.

Park by pulling down the prop stand and leaning the scooter over to the left to rest on it. If the handlebars are turned fully to the left they can now be locked in this position to guard against theft (*see* Fig. 18). In some respects this is a dubious virtue. Certainly the machine, as locked in this position, can virtually only be removed by carrying it away bodily, but the handlebar lock commonly becomes awkward to operate. To engage the key properly the lock itself has to be pushed in and the key turned. It is then often found difficult to *unlock* again.

CHAPTER IV

REGULAR MAINTENANCE

THE life of any machine is directly related to the care and attention it receives in the way of regular maintenance. Maintenance is not a technical subject for engineers only. It starts right away with the fuel mixture used to fill the tank and then embraces simple, regular checks and attention to lubrication of the various parts of the scooter, and simple adjustments to be made to improve the operating efficiency of the machine. Nothing about routine maintenance involves any special skills. Any owner can attend to this subject, and *must* attend to it, in fact, if costly repair bills are to be avoided at a later stage.

Engine lubrication is provided by SAE 40 grade oil mixed with the petrol in the tank. The reliability of a branded oil is unquestioned, thus it is only common sense to specify and stick to a well-known brand, asking for SAE 40 grade, or equivalent. It is suggested also, as general practice, that the same oil should be used throughout the life of the engine. This does not infer that the quality of these oils differs, merely that some may contain certain additives not found in others and slightly affect performance on an engine tuned to a particular mixture. This is not an important point, however.

The proportion of SAE 40 oil to petrol is *always* 1 pint of oil per $2\frac{1}{2}$ gallons of petrol for new engines or operating under heavy loads; or 1 pint of oil per 3 gallons of petrol for normal running. The corresponding oil-petrol ratios are 1:20 and 1:24, respectively.[1] No mixture should be used outside this specified range despite advice which may be offered to the contrary; for example, ignore the expert who claims an increase in performance or more miles per gallon using a lower oil proportion or a thinner oil than SAE 40. You could use an SAE 30 oil by increasing the oil ratio to about 1:16 but you will gain nothing in performance, spend more on oil and run the risk of invalidating any guarantee. At present, too (1960) the NSU guarantee is invalidated by the use of molybdenum disulphide lubricant additions.

Petrol and oil should always be mixed as described in Chapter III. When filling the tank, add the petrol first, then the oil, with the fuel tap turned off. Shake the machine to mix. If the mixing is done in a separate container it is usually best to put the oil in first and then the petrol on top. Inverting the container end over end slowly several times will ensure complete dispersion of the oil through the petrol and a consistent mixture.

[1] Or equivalent when using special two-stroke mixtures.

REGULAR MAINTENANCE

Even when mixed there is a certain tendency for oil to settle out at the bottom of a petrol-oil mixture. Thus if a container of mixture has been standing for some time it will pay to agitate it to re-mix before filling the tank. The same applies to the mixture in the tank when the scooter has been left unused for a long time.

Running In. On new engines moving parts are set up with small clearances and with possible high spots, quite microscopic in size, left by the final machine-finishing operation. These have to wear off until rubbing surfaces are smoothed and polished before friction is reduced to a minimum. This is something that cannot be prefabricated in making the parts. Only actual running will bed down the moving parts to an optimum sliding or rubbing fit.

Because of this possibility of "tightness" it is obviously important to treat the engine kindly during the first part of its life, make sure that it receives adequate lubrication (which is the reason for the higher oil proportion specified for running in), is not allowed to labour (which places more load on the bearings) or run flat out at full throttle (when the friction may generate heat to a damaging level). Contrary to popular opinion, it is *not* harmful to make a two-stroke engine work reasonably hard during the running-in period and continual very slow running or running at low speeds is doing no good at all, and may even be harmful to the bearings. The main points to observe are to stick within the speed ranges recommended for running in, always to change down in good time before the engine can start to labour under load, and to restrict the running load as much as possible during the first 500 miles. It is not advisable, for instance, to carry a pillion passenger until the engine is properly run in.

Recommended Running-in Speeds

Prima D: first gear   12 m.p.h.
           second gear   20–22 m.p.h.
           top gear   35 m.p.h.

Prima V: first gear   10 m.p.h.
           second gear   15–17 m.p.h.
           third gear   25 m.p.h.
           top gear   35 m.p.h.

Prima III: first gear   10 m.p.h.
            second gear   17 m.p.h.
            third gear   25 m.p.h.
            top gear   35 m.p.h.

Actually, too much emphasis is often placed on running-in speeds by the new driver. It is quite unnecessary to watch the clock so that recommended running-in speeds are not exceeded in any gear. It is far more important to avoid letting the engine run heavily loaded in any gear and at any speed. Change down early when ascending hills and avoid running

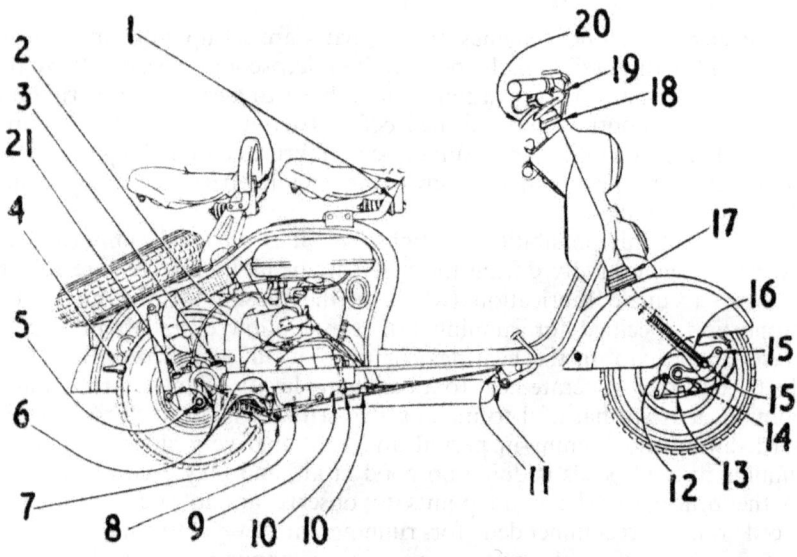

FIG. 19. LUBRICATION POINTS, PRIMA D

1. Saddle pivot
2. Gearbox oil filler
3. Grease filler plug, rear suspension
4. Side panel catches
5. Rear brake adjuster and rear wheel sprung mount
6. Rear brake rod support, lever bearing, shock absorber pivots
7. Front bearing rear wheel springing
8. Gearbox drain plug
9. Gearbox oil level plug
10. Clutch operating cable
11. Footbrake pedal oil rod support
12. Front brake adjuster
13. Front brake cable
14. Front wheel hub
15. Front suspension bearing and ball cup (front spring)
16. Front springs
17. Lower steering front
18. Upper steering front
19. Handlebar cable front and throttle twist-grip
20. Clutch lever front and gear control twist-grip
21. Grease filler plug rear wheel bearing

slowly under load in a high gear. The less *hard* work the engine has to do at relatively low speeds when new, the better for it.

After 500–600 miles the engine should be fully run in and capable of developing maximum power at full throttle for continuous operation.

Tyre Pressures. The life of the tyres as well as the stability and handling characteristics of the scooter will depend on keeping the tyre pressures close to recommended figures.

These are—   Front Tyre   Rear Tyre
   Prima D (solo)   18 lb per sq in.   20 lb per sq in.
     (with pillion passenger)   18 lb per sq in.   23 lb per sq in.
   Prima V (solo)   18 lb per sq in.   22 lb per sq in.
     (with pillion passenger)   18 lb per sq in.   25 lb per sq in.
   Prima III KL (solo)   18 lb per sq in.   22 lb per sq in.
     (with pillion passenger)   18 lb per sq in.   24 lb per sq in.

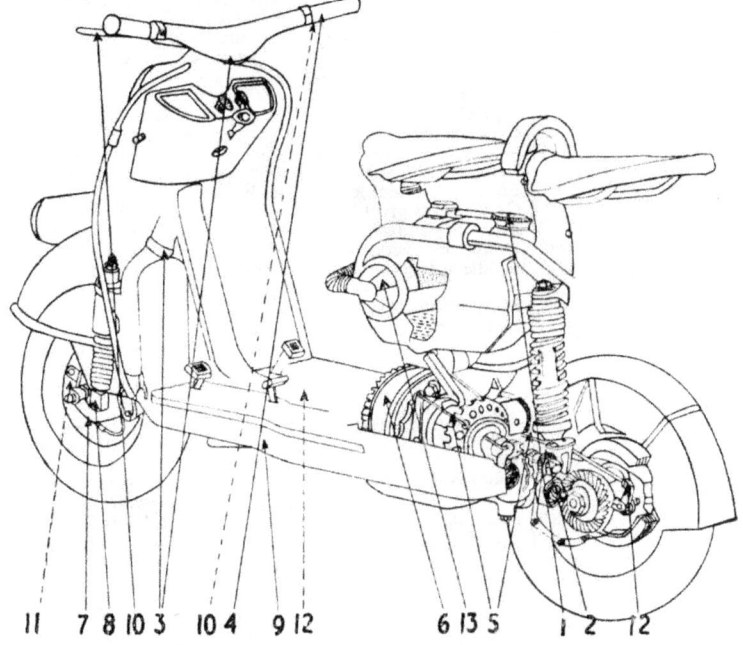

FIG. 20. LUBRICATION POINTS, PRIMA V AND III KL

1. Engine
2. Gearbox
3. Steering head bearings
4. Throttle twist-grip
5. Control cables
6. Contact-breaker pad
7. Speedometer drive
8. Front wheel bearings
9. Prop stand
10. Brake and clutch levers
11. Front brake cam lever
12. Front brake pedal pivot and linkage
13. Air cleaner

Regular Lubrication. Various parts of the machine require lubrication with oil or grease at stated intervals. These intervals are largely arbitrary but should be adhered to as far as possible, if only to get into the habit of appreciating that *regular* attention is important rather than spasmodic attention when it seems needed. For convenience lubrication requirements can best be summarized in a table, with the various lubrication points requiring attention illustrated in Fig. 19 for the Prima D and Fig. 20 for the Prima V and III KL.

LUBRICATION TABLE, PRIMA D
(*See* Fig. 19 for reference points, etc.)

When	Reference	Part(s) to be Lubricated	Lubricant and Remarks
—		Engine	Continuously lubricated by oil mixed with petrol in tank. Use only SAE 40 oil and 20:1–24:1 petrol-oil mixture
Weekly (or every 500 miles)		Grease nipple in cover plate Choke slide control cable	High-pressure grease (*See* special note 1, page 39) Oil with thin machine oil[1]
Monthly (or every 1,000 miles)	11 20 6 15 21 4 10, 19, 20	Foot pedal linkage Front brake cam lever Clutch lever pivot Brake lever pivot Front suspension Saddle springs Saddle front bearing Side panel catches Control cables	Two points to be oiled[1] Oil[1] Oil[1] Oil[1] Two points to be greased Apply grease to saddle springs and saddle ball joints Oil[1] Oil[1] Oil ends of cables with thin oil or petrol-oil mixture. Grease ends of cables where they emerge from sheathing
Three-monthly (or every 2,000–3,000 miles)	2 14 21	Gearbox Front wheel hub Rear wheel swinging arm and rear transmission	Drain and refill with SAE 30 oil (*See* special note 2, page 40) Two or three shots of high-pressure grease in nipple Shell Retinax G grease or equivalent. (*See* special notes 3 and 4, page 40)
Six-monthly (or every 5,000 miles)	 17, 18 3, 21	Throttle and gear-change twist-grips Steering head bearings Contact-breaker lubricating pad Rear transmission	Remove, smear with high-pressure grease and replace Check, clean bearing and repack with high-pressure grease, if necessary Smear with a thin layer of bearing grease (*See* special note 4, page 40)

[1] SAE 30 oil is recommended for all oiling points attended to with an oilcan but any good quality machine oil should be satisfactory. To lubricate cables, oil thinned with petrol can be dripped into the ends of the cable sheathing, after first disconnecting the cables. This will penetrate more readily than oil alone and can be continued until oil commences to drip from the lower ends of the cable sheathing.

REGULAR MAINTENANCE

LUBRICATION TABLE, PRIMA V and III
(*See* Figs. 20, 21 and 22 for reference points, etc.)

When	Reference	Part(s) to be Lubricated	Lubricant and Remarks
	1	Engine	Continuously lubricated by oil mixed with petrol. Use only SAE 40 oil and 20:1–24:1 petrol-oil mixture
Weekly (or every 500 miles)	5	Cables, if necessary	E.g. in wet weather, etc., otherwise attend to monthly
Monthly (or every 1,000 miles)	12 14 10 10 9 5	Footbrake lever Front brake cam lever Brake lever pivot Clutch lever pivot Side and prop stand Control cables	Oil[1] cable connector Oil[1] Oil[1] Oil[1] Grease bearing points Oil ends of cables and then grease ends where they emerge from sheathing
Three-monthly (or every 2,500 miles)	2 7	Gearbox Speedometer drive	Change oil Grease applied to nipple
Six-monthly (or every 5–6,000 miles)	4 3 15 6	Throttle twist-grip Steering head Front wheel hub Contact-breaker pad	Remove, smear with grease and replace Check, clean bearing and repack with high-pressure grease, if necessary Repack with high-pressure grease Smear with thin layer of grease

[1] See footnote on p. 36.

ROUTINE MAINTENANCE

The check list on page 39 is recommended as a pattern for regular inspection and maintenance. Certain items which require semi-skilled attention at the higher mileage figures are well within the capabilities of the average owner and need not be done by a garage. Complete details relative to these operations will be found in the subsequent chapters dealing with detailed maintenance.

It is important to appreciate that regular care and attention to the points listed not only minimizes deterioration but keeps the vehicle more efficient and safer and more pleasurable to drive. Points which should receive regular attention but are neglected can lead to progressively increasing wear and loss of efficiency. Simple maintenance costs are negligible, and the time involved usually low. It is only common sense to follow such a pattern of regular maintenance.

It is important to remember that before applying oil or grease at the various lubrication points the points involved, particularly the grease nipples, should be cleaned off with a rag. It is equally important to use

Fig. 21. Forward Plug Lubricates Rear Wheel Swinging Arm, Rear Plug Rear Wheel Transmission

Fig. 22. Gearbox Oil Filler (arrowed)
A regular oil change is specified. Model III KL shown. Prima V is similar

REGULAR MAINTENANCE

When	Item	Remarks
Weekly (or every 500 miles)	Air filter (ref. 13, Fig. 20)	Remove and clean by washing through with petrol. Blow dry, then lightly oil and replace
	Tyre pressures	Check for correct pressure and reinflate, as necessary
Monthly	Check battery	Get battery recharged, if necessary In winter a weekly check of the battery condition may be advisable Check level of electrolyte and top up with distilled water, if necessary
	Clutch	Check movement and adjust, as necessary—*see* Chapter VI
	Gear change	Check movement and adjust as necessary—*see* Chapter VI
	Wheel nuts	Check for tightness
	Cylinder head nuts	Check for tightness (when engine is cold)
	Steering head	Check for tightness
	Silencer fixing	Check for tightness
	Brakes	Check and adjust, as necessary
Three-monthly (or every 2–3,000 miles)	Decarbonize silencer	*See* Chapter VI
	Engine mount	Check for tightness, also upper and lower spring attachment points
	Sparking plug	Clean and adjust gap
Six-monthly (or every 4–5,000 miles)	Decarbonize cylinder head	*See* Chapters VI, VII and IX
	Clean Dynastart unit	*See* Chapter XI
	Check contact break gap	Adjust as necessary—*see* Chapter VI
	Check electrical wiring	Make good, as necessary
Every 10,000 miles	Sparking plug	Replace with new plug—*see* Chapter XII

only the recommended grade or type of lubricant as the *wrong* lubricant may do more harm than good.

Special Notes Applicable to the Prima D. *Note* 1. On some models there is no grease nipple on the cover plate, the left-hand outer crankshaft bearing receives lubrication via the oil in the petrol-oil mixture.

Note 2. The correct method of lubricating the rear transmission is to raise the rear wheel clear of the ground, start the engine and engage first gear. With the two filler plugs (*see* Fig. 21) removed grease is forced into the *forward* opening until it is visible through the *rear* opening. Do not add any more grease as an excess may be forced past the oil seal and penetrate into the rear brake.

Use only Shell-Retinax G, Mobil Epix or equivalent grease for the rear transmission. *On no account* use oil or a high-pressure grease.

Note 3. The gearbox must never be *overfilled* with oil as this may lead to a sticking clutch or an oiled-up rear brake. The correct level is indicated when oil is just beginning to drip out of the overflow hole.

Note 4. The correct procedure for renewing the grease in the rear transmission casing is to force new grease into the forward opening until all the old grease has been driven out through the rear opening—indicated by the fact that the grease finally emerging is clean and fresh. Then *withdraw some of the grease* so that the casing does not remain overfilled —*see* Note 2 above.

Special Note Regarding New Machines. In the case of new machines —or machines fitted with a new engine—it is good practice to drain and refill the gearbox after the first 250 miles running, and again after 500 miles. Subsequent oil changes should then be carried out at 2,000–3,000-mile or three-monthly intervals, as per the standard schedule.

To drain the gearbox the engine should preferably be warm—this operation is best carried out shortly after a run, or after running up the engine. In the case of the Prima D, drain by removing the filler plug, drain plug and the oil level control plug (*see* Fig. 19). With the Prima V and III, remove the upper (filler) and lower (drain) plugs in the final drive housing (*see* Fig. 22). Collect the oil in a suitable tin or similar container and *throw away*. It is of no further use.

To fill, replace the drain plug and add fresh SAE 80 oil through the filler plug, adding oil until it just overflows from the oil level plug hole on the Prima D; or until the gearbox is full in the case of the Prima V and III. Capacity of the gearbox is 0·3 litres (just over ½ pint) for the Prima D and ¾ pint for the Prima V and III.

CHAPTER V

TRACING AND CURING FAULTS

FOR convenience of reference this chapter is divided into two tables. The first details faults associated with starting troubles of the kind most commonly experienced by the new owner, where the cause is usually a mistake on the part of the operator. The second table details faults which may develop at a later stage, associated with wear, lack of maintenance, etc.

It cannot be emphasized too strongly that regular maintenance along the lines detailed in the previous chapter will prevent many such faults developing. All models of the Prima are essentially trouble-free if looked after properly, but no machinery is completely foolproof nor can it be expected to have an indefinite life.

The tables aim to locate typical faults against cause and cure and are intended as a general guide for trouble-shooting. The more experienced owner or the trained mechanic will know where to look and what action to take, but many of the simpler faults which may develop can readily be dealt with by the inexperienced owner without incurring the service charges involved with professional attention. Reference should be made to other sections of the book for specific information on adjustment, dismantling, etc., where called for, consulting the index to locate the appropriate pages.

Experience is the best guide of all in fault-finding—not necessarily trained engineering skill but experience and familiarity with the machine itself. The more you know about your machine and the way it is intended to behave, the more readily you can recognize possible troubles and rectify them before they have developed into anything too serious. In the main this is simply a matter of regular attention to adjustment and lubrication. Parts which are adjusted correctly, and properly lubricated, will work better as well as minimize wear and strain on those parts, and related components.

If anything is obviously wrong it should be put right as soon as possible —and the *cause* of the trouble investigated, as far as possible.

Many faults are far from difficult to trace and put right—and in a good many cases both the "cause" and "remedy" are obvious and straightforward. Difficulty in fault-finding is usually a state of mind—assuming that it is a "mechanic's" job, when it probably is not. Get familiar with your machine—and with fault-finding—and you can drive with considerably more confidence.

ELEMENTARY STARTING FAULTS

Symptom	Cause or Source of Trouble	Remedy or Action Needed
Engine will not start	(i) Lack of petrol To prove: operate tickler or choke knob to see if petrol overflows from carburettor	(a) Check whether fuel tank is empty (b) Check whether fuel tap is turned on (c) Feed pipe or tap blocked
	(ii) Too much petrol To prove: depress tickler or operate choke knob and see whether petrol immediately overflows. In bad cases petrol will be overflowing from the carburettor without further choking	(a) Turn off petrol, open throttle and treat as a flooded engine—*see* Chapter III
	(iii) No spark	(a) Plug dirty, wet or fouled up—requires cleaning or, better, replace with new, clean plug (b) Fault (iii) may be combined with (ii). If the plug is wet, suspect also a flooded engine and treat accordingly
	(iv) Ignition failure	(a) Not likely, but this can be checked by removing the lead from the plug, holding about ¼ in. from the side of the cylinder and operating the starter. If a spark jumps from the lead, the fault lies with the plug or a flooded engine
	(v) Ignition fault	(a) Can develop after use. *See* following table
Engine starts but stops soon afterwards	(i) Lack of petrol	(a) Choke pushed in too soon in cold weather (b) Lack of fuel in tank (engine has started and run only on fuel remaining in carburettor) (c) Fuel tap turned off (as above)
	(ii) Ignition failure	(a) Wire broken or shaken loose (b) Spark plug fouled up by wet deposit in engine
	(iii) Water in petrol	(a) Water in tank or carburettor
	(iv) Too much oil in petrol	(a) Causing plug to foul. Will not happen with correct petrol:oil ratio
	(v) Weak mixture	(a) Air leak—e.g. carburettor loose
Engine stops suddenly after a reasonable run	(i) Any of the faults above	(a) *See* above
	(ii) Carburettor fault	(a) Float damaged and leaking (b) Float displaced
	(iii) Contact-breaker fault	(a) Points oiled up
Engine labours and lacks pulling power	(i) Mixture too rich	(a) Check whether choke has been left out (b) Float damaged or leaking (c) Jet needle loose (d) Float sticking (e) Air filter needs cleaning

GENERAL FAULTS

Symptom	Cause or Source of Trouble	Remedy or Action Needed
Engine runs badly	(i) Mixture	(a) Check as above
	(ii) Ignition	(a) Check plug, contact breaker gap and points
	(iii) Misfiring and running hot	(a) Look for air leaks (b) Check carburettor (c) Check type of plug
Engine lacks pulling power	(i) Mixture	(a) Check as above (b) Check cylinder head bolts
	(ii) Carboned up	(a) Silencer, cylinder head and engine need decarbonizing (Not necessarily all three—decarbonizing the silencer and cylinder head only may be completely effective)
	(iii) Ignition	(a) Check plug (b) Check contact-breaker (c) Check wiring, etc., if no spark
Engine noisy	(i) Mechanical fault	(a) Try to trace where the noise is coming from. An unusual noise is a forewarning of trouble and possible failure, so try to locate and remedy (b) A screaming noise is usually an indication of lack of lubrication and should be looked for at once without further running (c) Check engine mounting nuts for tightness
Engine becomes unduly hot; also lacks pulling power	(i) Mixture	(a) Too lean, check carburettor (b) Air leaks
	(ii) Mechanical fault	(a) Clutch slipping (b) Brakes binding
Noise (general)	(i) Rattling noise	(a) Probably a loose fitting—trace source and tighten up
	(ii) Excess noise from silencer	(a) Casing split (b) Silencer worked loose
	(iii) Whining noise from gears	(a) Incorrect meshing when set up after a repair, or due to heavy wear
	(iv) Whining noise from transmission	(a) As above
Gear change	(i) Stiff to operate	(a) Cable seizing—needs cleaning and oiling (b) Cable kinked (c) Twist-grip binding (Prima D only)
	(ii) Slips out of gear	(a) Cable kinked (not likely) (b) Cable stretched—adjustment required (e.g. with new tension spring)
Clutch	(i) Slips when in gear	(a) Requires adjustment (b) If adjustment does not cure, springs may be weak or clutch lining worn below usable limit calling for clutch replacement
	(ii) Does not engage	(a) Can be caused by a sticking cable
	(iii) Sticks	(a) Oil on clutch plates acting as an adhesive. Effect should disappear after a short while (b) Clutch wrongly adjusted

Symptom	Cause or Source of Trouble	Remedy or Action Needed
Brakes	(i) Poor stopping power	(a) Need adjustment (b) Linings worn beyond useful limit, requiring replacement (c) Oil on drums
	(ii) Stiff	(a) Lack of lubrication on cable or pivot bearings
	(iii) One brake more effective	(a) The front brake will normally seem more effective for stopping on dry surfaces. Use both brakes evenly for equalized wear
Excessive fuel consumption	(i) Brakes binding	(a) Check and adjust, if necessary—brake drums will be hot after a run and braking power poor
	(ii) Wrong mixture	(a) Check carburettor (b) Partially blocked air filter giving rich mixture
	(iii) Engine fault	(a) Engine requires decarbonizing (b) Blown gasket (c) Cylinder head loose
	(iv) Ignition fault	(a) Timing incorrect (b) Mechanical fault on contact breaker
No lights	(i) Disconnexion (ii) Faulty earth connexion (iii) Short circuit (iv) Fuse blown (III KL only)	(a) Broken leads (b) Clean and re-make, as necessary (c) Look for chafed, frayed or bare wires (d) Replace
Parking lights weak	(i) Weak battery	(a) Check and recharge, if necessary
	(ii) Fault on dynamo unit (battery not charging)	(a) See Chapter XII—section on lighting
Individual lights out of action	(i) Broken bulb	(a) Check and replace
	(ii) Disconnexion	(b) Look for broken wires, loose connexions, etc.
	(iii) Earthing	(c) Partially broken wires or damaged insulation
Electrical faults	General	Refer to appropriate wiring diagram to check through
Starter faulty	(i) Weak battery	(a) Check, recharge, if necessary
	(ii) Dynastart unit fault	(a) A job for a service agent, but see Chapter XI
Steering faulty	(i) Wrong tyre pressures	(a) Check, reinflate as necessary
	(ii) Steering head loose	(a) Check bearings and adjustment
	(iii) Steering head stiff	(a) As above
	(iv) Wheel loose	(a) Check wheel nuts

CHAPTER VI

DETAILED MAINTENANCE, GENERAL

THE following descriptions apply to all Prima models, differences between the various models being noted where necessary. Detailed maintenance specific to the Prima D and Prima V and III is dealt with in subsequent chapters. In effect, this chapter covers detailed maintenance which is well within the scope of the non-skilled owner and which can be tackled by him (or her) with confidence. Maintenance described in the later chapters is more of a workshop nature—the kind of jobs normally given over to a service agent but again well within the scope of the amateur with some background knowledge of basic engineering and the handling of engineering tools.

TOOL KITS

Standard tool kits supplied with each new machine provide a minimum of tools required for simple maintenance work. Since some may be lost, or missing in the case of second-hand machines, contents of the tool kits are listed under for reference.

Prima D

Box spanner 14 × 21 mm
Tommy-bar 7 mm ($\frac{9}{32}$ in.) 130 mm (5 in.) long
Allen key 10 DIN 911
Pliers
Screwdriver
Double-ended flat spanner 14 × 17 mm
Double-ended flat spanner 10 × 11 mm
Double-ended flat spanner 8 × 9 mm

Prima V and III

Box spanner 14 × 21 mm
Allen key 10 DIN 911
Pliers
Screwdriver
Double-ended flat spanner 17 × 19 mm
Double-ended flat spanner 10 × 11 mm
Double-ended flat spanner 8 × 9 mm
Plug spanner

It should be noted that the spanners are metric sizes and should be asked for, as such. In the metric system the size specified for nuts and bolts refer to the width of the hexagon across the flats and not, as in standard British practice, to the diameter of the bolt.

BATTERY CARE

Two 6-volt 12 amp-hour batteries are used on the Prima D, Prima V and Prima III, connected in series to give a 12-volt supply. One 6-volt 6·7 amp-hour battery is fitted to the kick-start Prima III K and III KL. On the Prima D the batteries are carried in the compartment behind the front legshield, immediately under the instrument panel (*see* Fig. 23). On the

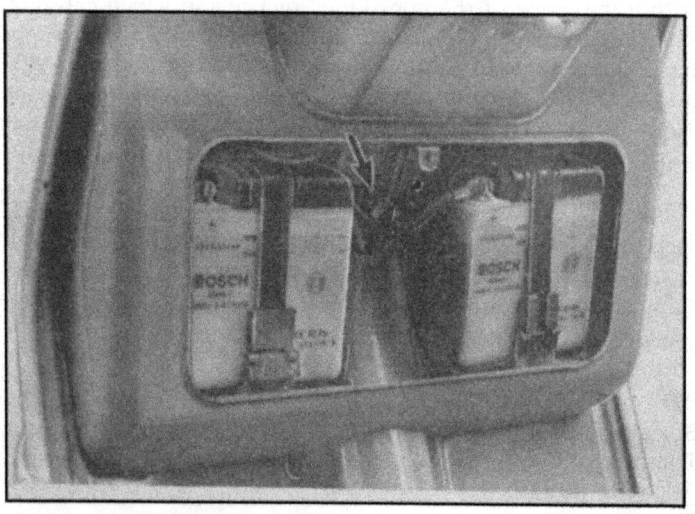

Fig. 23. Location of the Two 6-volt Batteries on the Prima D. Earth Terminal Arrowed

Prima V the two batteries are located on each side at the back of the frame—and on the III KL the single battery is positioned as shown in Fig. 52. In all cases the batteries are held in place by clamping straps.

Removal of the batteries in the case of the Prima D requires, first, disconnexion of the earth lead by unscrewing the earthing bolt on the frame. Push up the clips on the battery holder, using a screwdriver. Then push the battery and holder to the right or left, as appropriate, to take out. The metal straps can then be removed, also the two leads attached to the left hand battery (the main positive lead and the red coloured dynamo wire).

Replacement follows the reverse order exactly, always attaching the positive and dynamo leads to the battery before replacing and refitting

DETAILED MAINTENANCE, GENERAL

the earth lead last of all, carrying this cable over the top of the battery to reach the earthing bolt.

Battery removal on the Prima V and III is more or less obvious but must follow a similar order in that the negative (earth) lead is always removed *first* and replaced *last*.

If the scooter is required for running when the battery is removed (*see* Chapter III) the red dynamo lead must be attached to the main battery lead to complete the ignition circuit.

Main points to check in battery maintenance are that the acid level is

FIG. 24. SINGLE 6-VOLT BATTERY ON THE PRIMA III KL IS MOUNTED IN A SIMILAR POSITION TO THAT ON THE PRIMA III K, BUT ON LEFT-HAND SIDE ONLY

kept correct—just covering the plates as viewed from the top with the filler plugs removed. Dry, exposed plates will sulphate up and reduce the capacity of the battery. On the other hand, too high an acid level may result in some acid escaping through the vents with possible damage to the machine parts adjacent, or even to clothing should this come into contact with it. On later models (from No. 2 066226/3 355997 onwards) the batteries are enclosed in acid-proof bags, as standard. These are recommended for fitting to all machines.

Use only distilled water for topping up batteries. If any is spilt on to the casing, wipe dry with a clean cloth. Battery cases can be cleaned, if necessary, with a little water and wiped dry again. Battery terminals and lead spade clips should be kept clean and bright and protected with a light smearing of petroleum jelly or acid-resistant grease. Good, clean connexions are essential.

Battery recharging would normally be done by a garage. If, however, a home-charging unit is available, the recommended charging rate is 0·5 amp—not more. The battery on self-starter models has to do a lot of hard work, so it deserves proper care and attention in order to realize its full, useful life. Demand is also particularly high in winter weather. Damage can also result from failing to shut down the cover on the ignition switch when the key is removed. Moisture collecting inside this switch can lead to a short circuit which will quickly flatten the battery.

WHEEL CHANGING

To remove a front wheel the brake cable must first be disconnected—loosening the lock-nut and screwing the adjuster as necessary to release

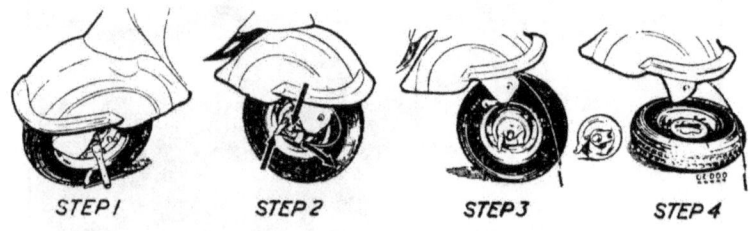

FIG. 25. FRONT WHEEL REMOVAL ON THE PRIMA D

the cable from the cam lever. The scooter, of course, will be supported on its prop stand or both stands, as appropriate.

The Prima D front wheel can then be removed by unscrewing both nuts on the front axle sufficiently so that the wheel can be dropped out (*see* Fig. 25). The hub can be detached from the wheel by removing the five domed nuts and washers.

The Prima V and III front wheel requires loosening of the coupling screws on either side of the forks, and removal of the hexagon nut on the left-hand side of the spindle. The spindle can then be knocked out to the right, allowing the wheel to drop. The speedometer drive housing must be detached from the left-hand side to release the wheel completely, also the front setscrew on the brake shackle on the right-hand side. The hub is detached from the wheel by removing the three domed nuts and associated spring washers.

Removal of the rear wheel requires removal of the left-hand side panel on the Prima D and the right-hand side panel on the Prima V and III. Unscrewing the cap nuts and washers (five on the Prima D, three on the Prima V and III) then allows the wheel to be lifted off the hub (*see* Figs. 26 and 27).

Replacement of a wheel follows the reverse order. It is very important that the spring washers be replaced under each cap nut and the nuts

Fig. 26. Unscrewing the Five Capped Nuts (arrowed) Allows the Prima D Rear Wheel to be Removed

The plain nuts must *not* be unscrewed with air in the tyre.

Fig. 27. Removal of Prima V Rear Wheel Requires Three Nuts only to be Unscrewed

tightened fully. Loose fitting can result in either the bolt holes tearing out or the studs themselves shearing.

Tyre Changing. The wheels are interchangeable (front to back) on any specific model, but not between models (the Prima V wheel, for example, is larger and of different form to that fitted to the Prima D). The Prima

FIG. 28. PRIMA D WHEEL (*left*) IS SPLIT-HUB CONSTRUCTION, PRIMA V AND III WHEEL (*right*) IS AN INTEGRAL PRESSING

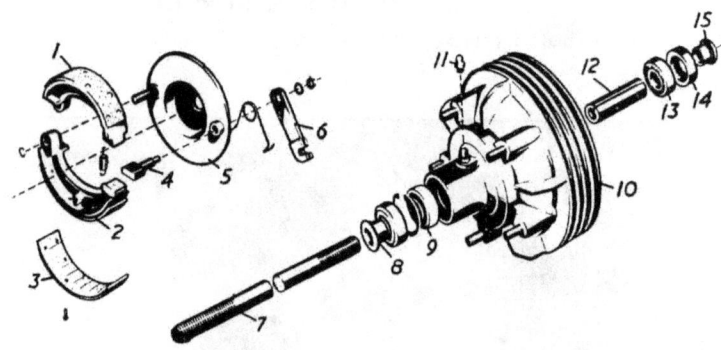

FIG. 29. FRONT WHEEL BRAKE, PRIMA D

1. Brake shoe and lining
2. Brake shoe
3. Brake lining (attached with 8 rivets each)
4. Brake cam
5. Brake backplate
6. Brake cam lever
7. Front axle (spindle)
8. Spacer bush and sealing ring
9. Ball bearing
10. Front hub
11. Grease nipple
12. Spacer tube
13. Ball bearing
14. Sealing ring
15. Spacer bush

D wheels are of split-hub construction bolted together by means of ten hexagon nuts (*see* Fig. 28). To remove a tyre *all the air must be let out first*—and this is very important—when the nuts can be undone and the two halves of the wheel parted. Always replace the split washers under the nuts when reassembling the wheel.

DETAILED MAINTENANCE, GENERAL

On the Prima V and III models the wheel is an integral unit with a deep well base rim (Fig. 28). The inner tube must be completely deflated to remove a tyre and the edge of the cover opposite the valve pressed right down into the well of the rim. It should then be readily possible to prise the edge of the cover on the valve side over the edge of the rim and hence remove the cover completely. Refitting follows the reverse order and again no great force should be necessary if the right technique is employed.

Spare Wheel. On the Prima D the spare wheel is removed by loosening the screws on the front of the luggage carrier, removing the wing nuts at the back and hinging the carrier up. The spare wheel can then be lifted off after removing the central domed nut holding the wheel disc and the three nuts holding the wheel on to its bracket.

To conform to the lighting regulations which became law in October, 1958, a modification of the rear lamp necessitated increasing the length of the rear carrier supports to provide enough clearance to accommodate the spare wheel under the carrier. Without these lengthened stays the increased length of rear lamp housing does not give sufficient clearance for the spare wheel to be fitted. The modification is standard on models subsequent to 2 073 137/3 362 954.

The Prima V and III spare wheel is simply released by unscrewing the wing nut under the centre of the wheel and sliding the wheel out sideways.

BRAKES AND CLUTCH

Front brake adjustment is done at the handlebar end of the cable where an adjuster is fitted. The lock-nut is loosened to free the adjuster which is then turned until the front wheel just spins freely without binding but the brakes begin to "bite" as soon as the brake lever is pulled. Lock this setting by tightening up the lock nut.

Rear brake adjustment on the Prima D is by means of a turnbuckle in the rear brake rod. Slacken off the lock-nuts at each end—noting that the rear lock-nut has a right-hand thread and the front lock-nut a left-hand thread, take up the adjustment as required by rotating the turnbuckle and then lock in this position by tightening the lock-nuts hard up on either side.

On the Prima V and III an adjuster is fitted at the front end of the cable sheathing under the running board. Free by loosening the lock-nut, take up adjustment as required, and then tighten the lock-nut.

Renewal of Brake Linings. The wheel must first be removed, as described above. In the case of the front wheel the brake backplate must be removed from the hub; and with the rear wheel the hub removed from the rear axle.

Removal of front wheel brake backplate: on the Prima D simply remove the nut on the backplate and take the backplate off complete with brake shoes. On the Prima V and III, knock out the bearing tube with a suitable mandrel or drift (e.g. a piece of hard wood) and lift off the backplate complete. (*See* Figs. 29, 30, 31, 32.)

Removal of rear hub: unscrew the central nut after bending back tab washer (Prima V and III only, the Prima D has a spring washer fitted as

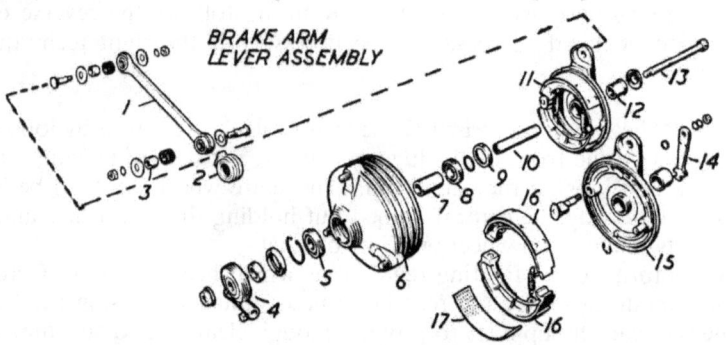

FIG. 30. PRIMA V FRONT WHEEL ASSEMBLY

1. Brake anchorage link
2. Cap
3. Bush
4. Speedometer drive
5. Ball bearing
6. Front hub
7. Bearing tube
8. Ball bearing
9. Oil seal
10. Spacer tube
11. Brake backplate (complete)
12. Bush
13. Axle spindle
14. Brake cam lever
15. Brake backplate (disassembled)
16. Brake shoe
17. Brake lining

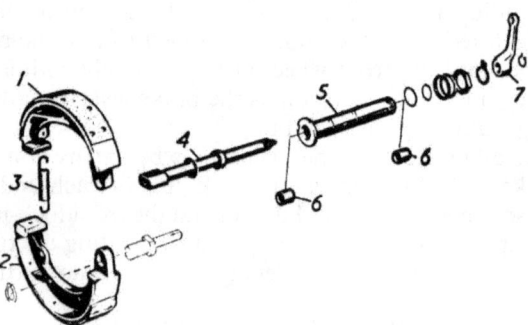

FIG. 31. REAR WHEEL BRAKE ASSEMBLY, PRIMA D

1. Brake lining
2. Brake shoe
3. Pull-off spring
4. Brake cam
5. Bearing bush
6. Bushes
7. Rear brake cam lever

standard). An extractor should then be used to withdraw the hub from the rear axle although if this special tool is not available the hub may be freed by striking the end of the axle with a block of hardwood (*not* a

DETAILED MAINTENANCE, GENERAL

metal hammer) at the same time pulling the hub forward. The nut can be replaced temporarily on the axle to guard the thread against damage.

Front hub and brake parts can be studied in Figs. 29 and 30, which indicate the manner in which the brake shoes are removed and subsequently replaced after fitting with new linings. The old linings can be removed with a cold chisel. New linings should be riveted in place at the centre first, using only standard replacement linings. Before reassembling grease the brake cam lightly with high-melting-point grease, also the return springs, taking care not to get any surplus grease on to the linings.

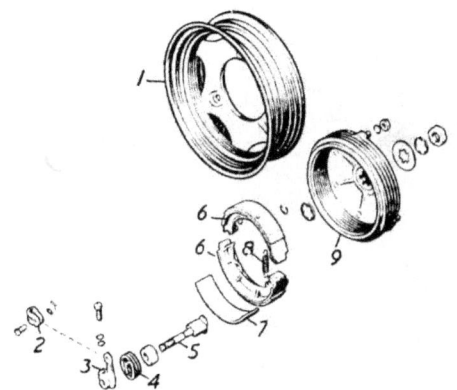

Fig. 32. Rear Wheel and Brake Assembly, Prima V

1. Rear wheel
2. Yoke
3. Brake cam lever
4. Spring
5. Brake cam
6. Brake shoe
7. Brake lining
8. Pull-off spring
9. Rear hub

On the Prima D the cones must be free from oil and grease when reassembled.

If the rear brake lever on the Prima D, Fig. 31, is removed for any reason it is important that it be reassembled in the same position as before —i.e. pointing upwards. It is best to mark the original position before taking off as if it is reassembled in a totally wrong position the brakes can jam on. The Prima V rear brake is detailed in Fig. 32.

Clutch. The adjuster for the clutch cable is on the bottom cable end underneath the right-hand footboard on the Prima D; and on the upper end of the cable adjacent to the clutch lever on the Prima V and III. Adjust, as necessary, until the clutch lever has a free movement or play of between $\frac{1}{32}$ in. and $\frac{1}{16}$ in. and make sure that the clutch operates properly over the full swing of the handlebars.

On the Prima D, pulling in the clutch lever also releases a locking device on the gear-change segment and for satisfactory operation of this other control there must be a clearance of 10 mm (just under ½ in.) behind the clutch lever (i.e. between it and the clutch cover plate). The gear-lock cable attached to the clutch lever has a separate adjuster and must be adjusted to have a play of about 1 mm (40 thou) when the clutch lever is pulled in.

Removal and replacement of the clutch can be done on all models without removing the engine from the frame. The Prima D clutch unit is shown in Fig. 33. Disassembly entails unscrewing the cap on the clutch, removing the sealing ring and then the two nuts from the operating rod

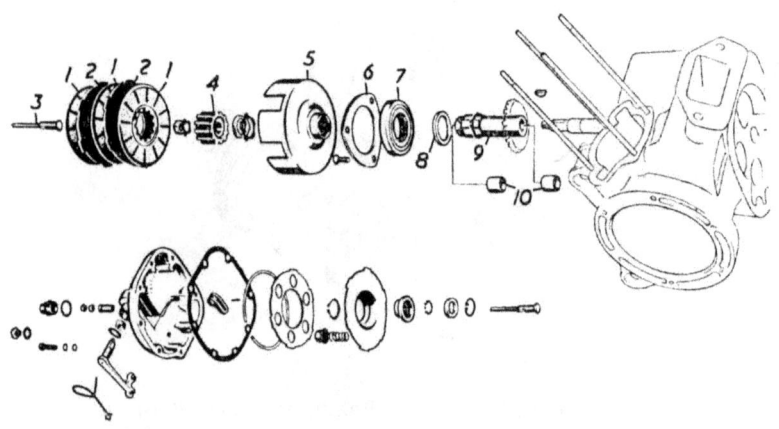

FIG. 33. THE PRIMA D CLUTCH

1. Lined clutch plate
2. Clutch plate
3. Clutch rod
4. Clutch centre
5. Clutch casing
6. Flange for ball bearing
7. Ball bearing
8. Shim
9. Driving shaft
10. Bearing bushes

so that the bush with spherical end can be withdrawn. An allen key is required to remove the clutch cover screws, when this unit can be taken off with its gasket. A special tool must now be used (see Chapter VIII) to screw on to the operating rod and tighten up to compress the clutch springs so that the spring clip can be prised off the rod with a small screwdriver or circlip pliers. The remaining parts can then be withdrawn in sequence, following the diagram, finally withdrawing the spindle by inserting a mandrel into the drive shaft bush and using the withdrawing tool located in the clutch housing. If necessary, the drive shaft itself can be freed by removing the ball race flange (held by three screws), knocking out the ball race and withdrawing the shaft complete with its shim.

For disassembly of the Prima V and III clutch, consult the exploded view given in Fig. 34. To gain proper access to the clutch it is necessary to remove the rear wheel and rear mudguard, release the clutch and rear

DETAILED MAINTENANCE, GENERAL

brake cables and undo the gear-change rods. Remove the slotted screw with spring washer on the bottom end of the rear wheel shock absorber and drive out the locking plate with a suitable mandrel, leaving the mandrel in position. This will allow the suspension to be pushed back out of the way so that the gear housing can be removed complete with rear wheel drive by undoing the nuts attaching it to the crankcase.

The special tool (*see* Chapter X) for compressing the clutch springs attaches to the crankcase with two nuts and, when screwed in, allows the circlip to be removed, followed by the pressure cup, springs and spring cups. The holder is then applied to the lined clutch disc, the lock plate

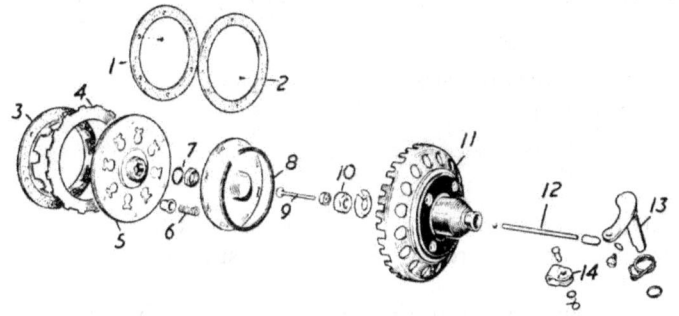

FIG. 34. THE PRIMA V CLUTCH (III KL CLUTCH IS SIMILAR)

1. Clutch plate
2. Clutch plate
3. Thrust plate
4. Clutch plate
5. Main plate
6. Clutch springs (8)
7. Lock plate and nut
8. Circlip for clutch cup
9. Thrust rod
10. Nut
11. Damper
12. Thrust rod
13. Lever
14. Yoke

tab pressed to release the nut which is then unscrewed. The large circlip is removed next, whence the lined disc can be withdrawn with an extractor (*see* Chapter X). Replacement follows in the reverse order, starting with the lined disc and supporting plate together. When refitting the gearbox and rear drive unit it is important to see that both the fitting sleeves mesh correctly and the clutch is properly engaged through the shock absorber. Fastening nuts around the housing should be tightened up from side to side, diagonal fashion, and not progressively around the periphery.

Changing the Clutch and Brake Cables. On the Prima D this necessitates removing the headlamp and cowling over the front forks when the clutch cable can be disconnected from the engine, the adjuster unscrewed and the nipple detached from the clutch lever. The brake cable is simply detached at each end. New cables can be drawn in by looping to the old cable with a piece of wire and pulling through as the old cable is withdrawn. The cable clips on the frame should be loosened to give free passage.

On the Prima V and III the front fairing must be removed, otherwise the procedure is the same. After being fitted new cables must, of course, be adjusted for correct operation of the controls as described above.

Removal of Twist-grip Controls. This is similar on all machines (*see* Fig. 35) except that the Prima V and III has only one twist-grip control (the throttle) on the right-hand handlebar. Pushing back the rubber

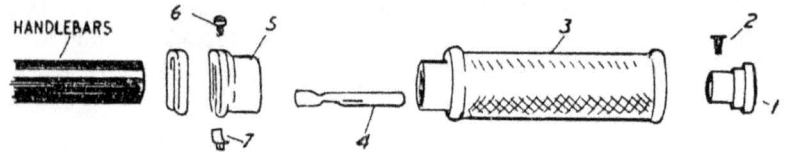

FIG. 35. HANDLEBAR TWIST-GRIP THROTTLE CONTROL (ALL MODELS)

1. End cap
2. Screw
3. Twist-grip sleeve
4. Slider
5. Body
6. Grub screw
7. Spring

sleeve on the grip exposes a countersunk screw which, when removed, allows the end cap to be removed and the twist-grip to be pulled off with an outward twisting motion.

The gear-change twist-grip (Prima D only) should be turned to second gear position to unscrew the countersunk holding screw and remove the

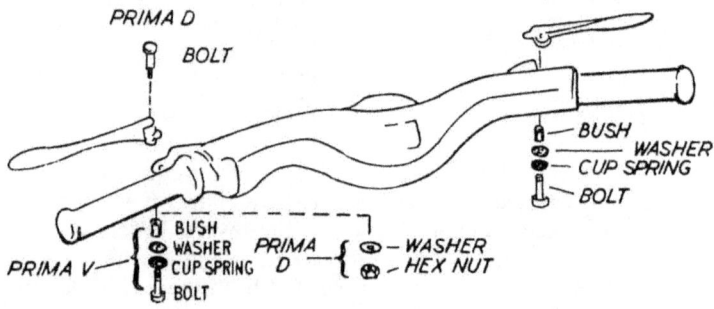

FIG. 36. CLUTCH AND BRAKE LEVER DETAILS

end cap, then rotated to third gear position. Disconnect the clutch cable at both ends, remove the screw and star washer on the underside of the twist-grip body to detach the cover when the segment carrying the gear-change cable can be taken off. The twist-grip can now be pulled off the handlebars.

Reassembly follows the same order, always replacing with third gear engaged and checking that the mark on the segment carrying the gear-change cable corresponds to the mark on the body of the twist-grip.

DETAILED MAINTENANCE, GENERAL

Clutch and Brake Levers (Fig. 36). The appropriate cable should first be detached from its lower end (i.e. on brake lever or clutch lever). Pulling the lever towards the handlebars will then expose the slot through which the cable can be detached from the lever. Unscrew the pivot bolt holding the lever, complete with washer and spring washer when the lever will

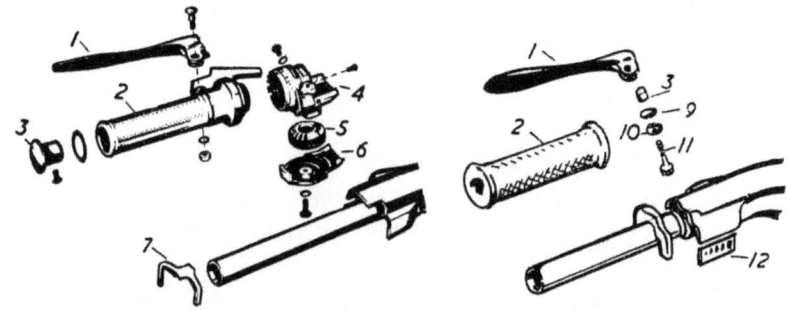

FIG. 36A. GEARSHIFT (*exploded*) PRIMA D (*left*), AND LEFT-HAND GRIP, PRIMA V (*right*)

Prima D 1. Clutch lever
         2. Grip
         3. End cap
         4. Body
         5. Roller
         6. Cap
         7. Edging strip

Prima V 1. Clutch lever
        2. Grip
        3. Bush
        9. Washer
       10. Cup spring
       11. Bolt
       12. Plate

come free. Replace washers, etc., in exactly the same order as they were removed (e.g. the cup spring the same way round on the brake lever assembly).

REPLACEMENT OF THROTTLE CABLE

This entails removal of the throttle twist-grip as described above. The throttle slide is then removed from the carburettor—*see* "Carburettor"—and the cable disengaged from it. A new cable can then be drawn into place as described for the brake and clutch cables.

STARTER CONTROL CABLE

To obtain complete access to the cable ends the headlamp and front cowling must be removed on the Prima D; and the front fairing and instrument panel on the Prima V and III. In the case of the Prima D the air inlet silencer must be taken off, the lever detached from the tickler by withdrawing the split pin and the cable adjuster unscrewed. At the instrument panel end pull out the choke knob, hold the spindle with pliers and unscrew the knob. Loosen the nut under the instrument panel and then unscrew the knurled nut on the top of the panel so that the sleeve and cable can be withdrawn, taking off the hexagon nut and bracket.

The new cable is fitted from the engine side, reassembling in the reverse order.

On the Prima V and III, releasing the instrument panel to allow it to tilt backwards makes it easy to detach the cover plate on the instrument panel and proceed to release the cable from this end. The carburettor should be detached from the engine by loosening the clamping bolt when it can be swung to one side and the cable guide detached from the mixing-chamber housing complete with spring and plunger. The old cable can then be detached and a new one fitted, by drawing it up into position with the old cable, pulled out from the top end.

GEAR-CHANGE CABLE (PRIMA D ONLY)

Two cables run to the gearbox although this is essentially a single cable doubling back around the segment fitted to the throttle twist-grip. To

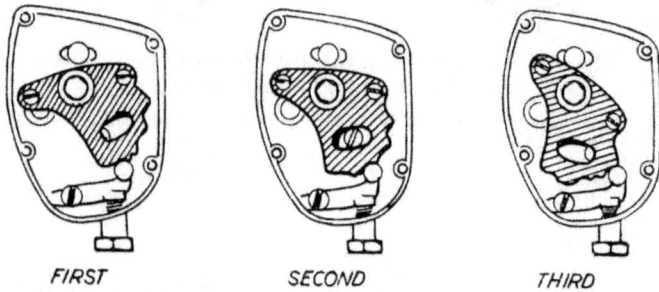

FIRST   SECOND   THIRD

Fig. 37. Alignment of the Gear Change (Prima D)

detach the cables from the gearbox end it is necessary to take off the gearbox cover plate, remove the split pins from the pivot pin and screw the cable adjusters right in so that the nipples can be freed. Loosen the adjusters again to pull the cables out in an upward direction.

Recommended practice for refitting is to insert the new cable from the front and attach to the gear-change twist-grip segment first. Then engage bottom gear and screw the adjuster of the shorter of the two cable ends into the front hole in the casing, the other one into the rear position. Locate both nipples and refit the split pins. Second gear should be selected on the twist-grip and on the gear-change mechanism in the gearbox (see Chapter VII) and both adjusters taken up until there is no play in either of the cables.

Adjustment of the gear change is shown in Fig. 37. The position of the locking pin in top and bottom gears is particularly important. The gear casing can be released for adjustment by slackening the countersunk screws. In neutral position, and rotating the rear wheel to drive the output shaft, a clicking should develop if the casing is moved slowly to the right.

DETAILED MAINTENANCE, GENERAL

If the casing is then moved back slightly from this position it should be correct, when the screws can be tightened right up.

A more positive method is to rotate the casing slowly to the right until clicking is heard when the rear wheel is turned (equivalent to second gear just coming into engagement) and then to rotate the casing to the left to establish the amount of movement in neutral, i.e. until clicking starts on this side (corresponding to first gear just coming into engagement). The

FIG. 38. TURNBUCKLE PROVIDES ROUGH METHOD OF GEAR ADJUSTMENT ON PRIMA V AND III KL

Note that the two lock-nuts have right- and left-hand threads, respectively.

casing should then be adjusted to a position such that the distance between neutral and second gear is shorter than the distance between neutral and first gear and tightened up.

Correct *cable* adjustment is when the two cables are a firm but not too tight fit in their sockets in neutral gear position. Incorrect selection of gear-change position by the twist-grip control will be caused if the cable-carrying segment is not replaced correctly—the mark must correspond with the mark on the housing with the gear-change mechanism in third (top) gear.

Faults, such as jumping out of gear or being unable to select a particular gear readily, are a matter of adjustment at the gearbox end, as just described. It is possible, however, that the drive may tend to jump out of second gear, even with correct adjustments. The cause in this case will almost certainly be due to a weakening of the spring tensioning the locking pin against the ratchet plate and a new or stronger spring should be fitted.

PRIMA V and III GEAR CHANGE

The gear change on the Prima V and III is operated by a rocking lever with two footrests, operating on the gearbox via an intermediate lever and gear-change link. A turnbuckle in this rear link provides a means of adjustment (see Fig. 38) although this will prove very much a trial-and-error method for any owner not familiar with gearbox operation. Initial adjustment or setting up is done on an eccentric bolt, by turning it slightly to the left or right, as necessary, until moving the gear lever into change positions audibly engages in first, second and third gears, then by tightening up the lock-nut to lock at this setting. No further adjustment should be necessary and, if apparently called for, is most likely due to excessive wear or to a fault developing in the gearbox itself, calling for a strip down (see Chapter IX).

CARBURETTOR

The carburettor fitted to the Prima D is a Bing model 1/20/22; to the Prima V either a Bing 1/24/109 or Bing 1/29/112; and to the III a Bing model 1/22/105. These units are fully described in Chapters VII and IX dealing with the Prima D and Prima V and III engines, respectively, with specifications in Chapter I.

Sparking Plug. Standard plug specified for the Prima D is a Bosch W 225 T 11; and the Prima V and III a Bosch W 190 M 11S. Suitable British equivalents are—

	Prima D	Prima V	Prima III
Lodge	H.H.14	H.H.14	H.H.14
Champion	L 10S	L 10S	L 10S
K.L.G.	F 80	F 80	F 80

Plug gap should be set at 0·024 inches (0·6 mm) for most consistent performance. A little more or less will not usually matter, but it is just as easy to set correctly as to any other figure. Since there may be a tendency for the gap to change slightly in use it is good practice to check regularly and re-set as necessary. This is done by prising open or tapping closed the side electrode *gently* to arrive at the desired gap setting as measured with a feeler gauge. As an emergency measure for setting the gap, an ordinary cigarette packet is usually about 0·012 inches thick card, so two pieces laid together will give a "feeler gauge" of about the right thickness.

It is equally important to keep the plug clean, again removing the plug at regular intervals for this purpose—see Regular Maintenance, Chapter IV. The optimum life of a plug in a two-stroke engine, too, is limited to about 10,000 miles running. It may go on working apparently satisfactorily for long after this, but its efficiency will be low and scooter performance and fuel consumption may be adversely affected.

DETAILED MAINTENANCE, GENERAL

For proper operation of the engine, too, the spark for igniting the fuel mixture in the cylinder must maintain or reach the correct temperature, governed mainly by the design of the engine. Also the body of the plug must maintain a satisfactory temperature. If the plug gets too hot it may cause pre-ignition of the fuel. If too cold, then oil from the petrol-oil mixture may condense on the points resulting in a fouled plug and a weak or no spark.

This is the reason why a particular type of sparking plug is specified for a particular engine. It has shown, on test, to have satisfactory operating characteristics for that engine. Other types of plug—equally

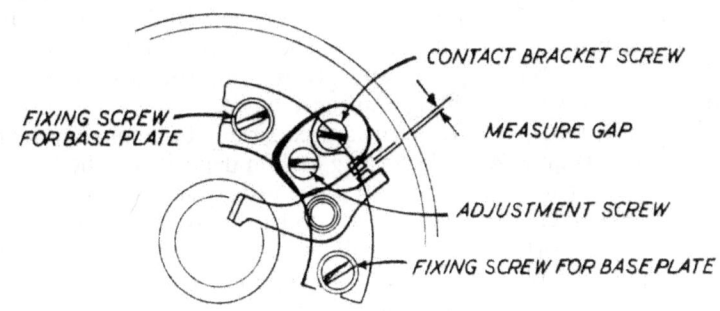

FIG. 39. CONTACT-BREAKER ADJUSTMENT IS MADE BY SLACKENING SCREWS INDICATED

efficient in their own operation—may not be suited for that particular engine. Hence the reason for sticking to a recommended type, as this should give trouble-free operation. A correctly balanced plug will still soot up but the deposit formed will be a uniform grey in appearance. If the plug is too "soft" for the engine the electrodes will become heavily corroded with a whitish deposit. Conversely, if the plug is too "hard" the deposit formed will be very black and oily in appearance. Either of these characteristics appearing on a standard plug indicate that the mixture is wrong—check carburettor settings.

Contact-breaker. The contact-breaker on the Prima D is reached for adjustment by removing the cover plate and turning the flywheel, as necessary, to expose the points. The correct gap setting for these is 0·014 to 0·016 inches, with the arm on the highest point of the cam, i.e. the points fully open.

If adjustment is necessary loosen the bolt holding the contact-breaker bracket (see Fig. 39) and turn the adjusting screw with a screwdriver until the gap is correct—measured with a clean feeler gauge. Then tighten up the first bolt, taking care that the adjustment is not disturbed.

The two screws, one at each end of the contact-breaker baseplate, are used only for adjusting the ignition timing and must not be touched in adjusting the points. For details on adjusting the *timing*, see Chapter XI.

DECARBONIZING

Decarbonizing is a relatively straightforward job. The need for it occurs since the burning fuel inevitably deposits soot or carbon inside the engine and silencer which eventually become so thickly coated that the proper gas flow is no longer maintained. Heavy carbon deposits inside the cylinder head, too, may heat up into localized "hot spots" causing pre-ignition of the mixture. The usual sign that decarbonizing is called for is a falling off in power with the engine otherwise running normally.

The silencer usually requires decarbonizing first and is easy to tackle simply by removing it from the machine, dismantling it completely, scraping off all carbon deposits and giving a thorough cleaning to all internal parts, then reassembling and replacing it.

The engine can be partially decarbonized simply by removing the head (*see* Chapters VII and IX) and scraping carbon deposits off the head with a piece of stick or a similar soft tool. The top of the cylinder above the piston can also be cleaned out; try not to leave any loose carbon inside, or in the exhaust port opening. It will probably be found that this latter opening is partially blocked with carbon deposits and so obviously needs attention when it has been made accessible.

LAYING A SCOOTER UP

If a scooter is laid up for any length of time it should be raised on its two stands to take the weight off the suspension and tyres and the battery should be removed. The latter should be kept fully charged and topped-up, being recharged at monthly intervals. It is better to use the battery, if possible, so that it continues to run through normal charge and discharge cycles. If the battery is left to stand in a flat condition it will quickly become ruined. If left to stand fully charged it is not likely to deteriorate much, but it will slowly lose that charge and so require recharging at intervals, as already specified.

The engine should not come to any harm on standing, but as a safeguard the plug can be removed and a little oil—preferably inhibiting oil—dropped in through the plug hole. Turn the engine over to dispense this oil over the surface of the cylinder and piston. The plug should not be replaced as this could cause the cylinder to "sweat" internally. The plug hole should be stopped up with a *loose* plug of gauze or a similar semi-porous bung to keep dirt out but still to allow the cylinder to breathe.

As to the rest of the machine, deterioration of frame parts, etc., is far less likely if the scooter is cleaned thoroughly before being laid up and then stored under cover and under wraps (e.g. covered over with a dust sheet).

CHAPTER VII

THE PRIMA D ENGINE

THE complete engine unit comprises the engine and flywheel, transmission casing, rear suspension unit and rear hub. The whole can be dropped out of the frame for convenience of working on the engine, etc., or for a major overhaul, although the following partial strip-downs can be done with the engine mounted in the frame, if preferred, but, in this case, the tank must be removed first—

1. Removal of cylinder head (e.g. for decarbonizing).
2. Removal of cylinder barrel.
3. Removal of clutch.
4. Removal of flywheel magneto generator and starter.

To remove the engine complete, the following must be done first—

(a) Take off both side panels.
(b) Remove the foot rests.
(c) Take off the complete exhaust system (using "C" spanner for undoing cylinder joint).
(d) Detach the high tension lead from the spark plug.
(e) Remove the fuel pipe.
(f) Loosen the clamping bolt on the carburettor and slide off.
(g) Detach gear-change and clutch cables.
(h) Remove rear wheel.
(i) Remove rear mudguard.
(j) Detach the shock absorber from the rear suspension by undoing the fixing screw.
(k) Remove circlip and split pin from rear brake intermediate lever and main lever, respectively.
(l) Slacken holding screws and pull off air ducts from engine.
(m) Detach speedometer drive.
(n) Finally remove toolbox, cowling around engine and remove the tank by twisting out in a clockwise direction.

Before the engine can be dropped it will be necessary to remove the central stand, making provision for the frame to be properly supported by some other means. The spring on the stand can be disengaged from one end, the pivot bolt removed and the stand taken off. Replace the bolt temporarily with a suitable pin. The side "prop" stand is bolted to the main frame and need not be removed.

The engine is held only by the two nuts on the side of the frame, the studs in the engine casing fitting into slots in the fixing lugs. When these nuts are slackened off, therefore, the engine will drop out suddenly unless supported or held by the swinging link and lowered gently. It is also important to note that the wedging rings, fitted in the slotted lugs, are merely held with grease. These are used to align the engine when remounting and must not be lost or damaged.

Special tools (*see* Chapter VIII) include an engine mounting stand on which the detached engine can be fitted for convenience of further working.

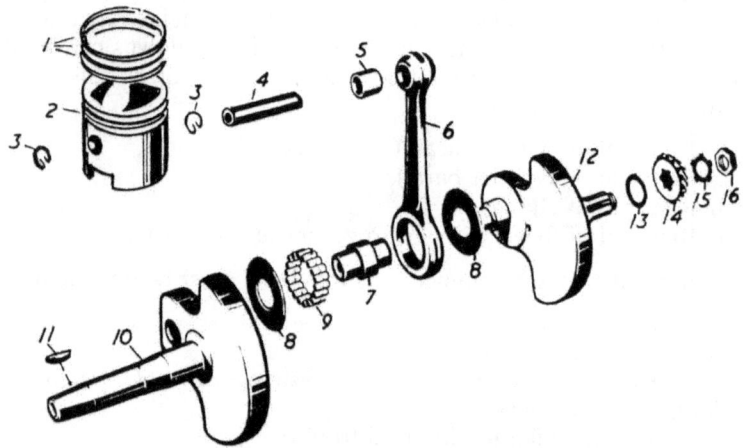

FIG. 40. CRANKSHAFT ASSEMBLY, PRIMA D

1. Piston rings
2. Piston
3. Circlips
4. Gudgeon-pin
5. Little end bush
6. Connecting rod
7. Crank pin
8. Thrust washer

9. Rollers (36)
10. Crankshaft (starter side)
11. Key
12. Crankshaft (drive side)
13. Shim for bevel pinion
14. Bevel pinion on crankshaft
15. Locking plate (star washer)
16. Nut

Otherwise the engine can be laid on a bench or suitably supported by blocks, etc., as necessary.

The cylinder head is held by four nuts with washers underneath. The cylinder barrel can be lifted up off the studs when the head is removed. A gasket is fitted to the top and bottom of the barrel and these may require replacement when reassembling. To remove the piston the two spring clips on each end of the gudgeon-pin bearing must be removed with pliers and the piston heated gently, when the gudgeon-pin can be driven out. It is too tight a fit to remove cold without fear of damage. When working on the engine in this state it is advisable to plug or cover the hole in the crankcase with a clean cloth to prevent dirt, etc., dropping inside the crankcase.

THE PRIMA D ENGINE

The rear wheel drive complete with suspension can be removed after first draining all the oil from the crankcase. It is held on with ten allen-head screws but before attempting to remove it the gearbox change mechanism should be set to third (top) gear position. The pin must also be driven out, after first removing the circlip. The rear wheel unit is then lifted off, holding the gearbox ratchet place in position to prevent third gear from dropping out and spilling the needle rollers.

The clutch is removed as described in Chapter VI, followed by the drive shaft. This leaves the right-hand side of the engine "bare." The flywheel

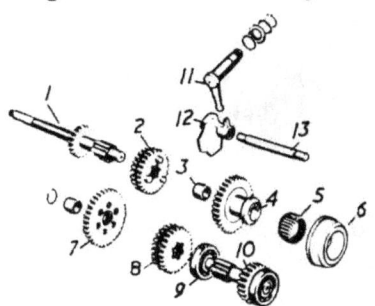

FIG. 41. PRIMA D GEARBOX

1. Gearbox main shaft (with 18 tooth pinion)
2. Sliding pinion (27 teeth)
3. Bush
4. Pinion (32 teeth)
5. Needle rollers (24)
6. Outer race for needle rollers
7. Pinion (35 teeth
8. Sliding pinion (26 teeth
9. Ball race
10. Layshaft
11. Gear-change lever
12. Selector fork
13. Gear-change spindle

dynamo-starter on the left-hand side is partially stripped by removing the circlip holding the cover plate, taking off the cover plate and undoing the bolt holding the fan. Component parts of the whole assembly are similar to those shown in Fig. 63.

If it is necessary to withdraw the dynamo unit this can be done by inserting a 2¾-in. long ¾-in. diameter pin and withdrawing with a suitable screw. The five screws and spring washers on the dynamo housing can then be removed and the housing pulled off complete once the brushes are lifted with the aforementioned pin and bolt.

Proceeding from there to remove the crankshaft, the locking plate on the left-hand side must be knocked out with a suitable drift and the nut then unscrewed and removed with its locking washer. This nut has a left-hand thread. The bearing cover can be loosened by tapping lightly with a block of wood, after first removing the holding screws. The crankshaft should then be turned to bottom dead centre position when it should be possible to knock it out from the left-hand side by hitting the right-hand end with a length of brass rod and a hammer. The bevel gear and shims will come away as well (*see* Fig. 40).

The ballraces are a light shrunk fit in the crankcase and can only be removed by heating the crankcase evenly and then tapping the crankcase against a wooden surface. New bearings must be shrunk fitted by being inserted in the heated crankcase.

When reassembling the crankshaft unit particular care must be taken to ensure that the correct meshing and backlash is obtained on the bevel gear set which, incidentally, are matched pairs of gears and cannot be replaced independently. The screws holding the ball bearing flange must be tightened evenly and should be checked by mounting the clutch bell

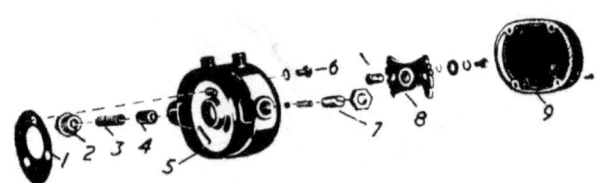

FIG. 42. PRIMA D GEAR-CHANGE UNIT

1. Protective disc
2. Plug
3. Helical spring
4. Locking pin
5. Gear-change casing

6. Screw and star washer (3)
7. Screw adjuster
8. Ratchet plate
9. Cover

and turning by hand to make sure that the shaft turns freely. If a dial gauge is available the backlash can be checked against the edge of one of the clutch bell cut-outs and should be of the order of 0·006 in. ($\pm$ 0·002 in.). Meshing can be checked by painting the gear teeth and then turning (by means of the clutch bell) to observe the gear teeth contact by the manner in which the paint is squeezed from the surface. Adjustment is carried out by adding or removing shims.

Gearbox. Component parts are detailed in Fig. 41 whilst gear-change adjustment has already been described (Chapter VI and Fig. 37). When you are disassembling second gear should be engaged and the sliding wheel, shaft, selector fork complete with countershaft and top gear wheel removed; be careful not to lose the needle rollers (24 in number). The drive shaft can then be pulled out with a pair of pliers.

In reassembling the 24 needles are fitted with grease into the direct gear wheel and placed in the outer ring of the drive casing. The drive shaft follows, being brought into the correct position by turning the rear wheel hub. The gear selector fork and spindle is then placed on the countershaft and the complete assembly inserted into the drive housing, the gear lever sliding into the recess on the gear selector fork. Replace the 27 teeth sliding pinion on the main shaft and mesh with the direct gear (18 teeth) by sliding inwards.

THE PRIMA D ENGINE 67

When the gearbox housing is replaced (*see* Fig. 42) the slots in the housing must be in line with the centre holes, the three countersunk screws (with conical star washers under) being only lightly tightened. Top gear is engaged and the gear-change ratchet plate fitted with the notch for top

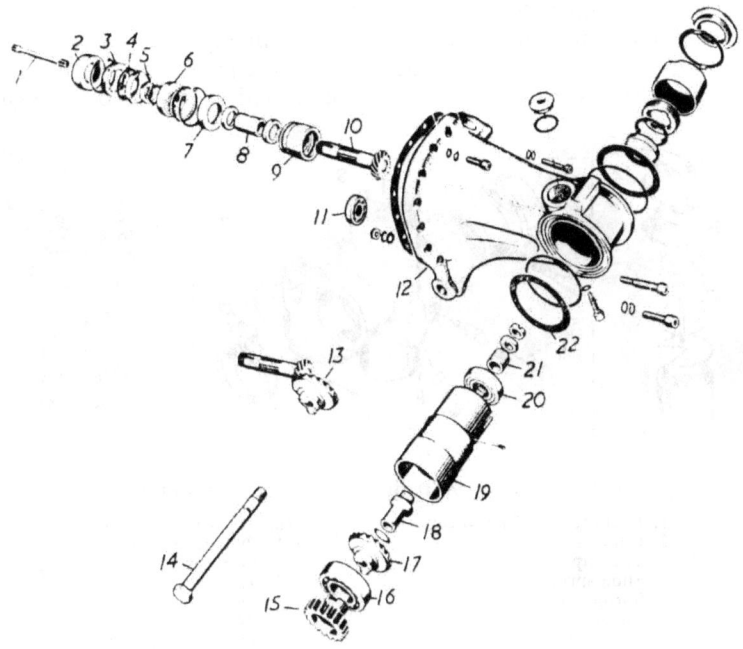

FIG. 43. PRIMA D REAR TRANSMISSION

1. Quill shaft
2. Outer race for needle rollers
3. Threaded insert
4. Locking plate
5. Locking plate and nut for bevel pinion
6. Ball bearing
7. Sealing ring
8. Spacer bush
9. Needle bearing
10. Rear bevel gear pinion
11. Ballrace for layshaft
12. Casing for intermediate gear
13. Rear transmission bevel gears
14. Bolt
15. Spur gear pinion (16 teeth)
16. Ball bearing
17. Crown wheel
18. Spacer bush with collar
19. Bearing bush for swinging arm
20. Ball bearing
21. Spacer bush
22. Shim

gear position pointing towards the operating lever. The segment is secured with a bolt, spring washer and large flat washer. Finally replace the helical spring tensioning the locking pin together with its stud and lock with a nut. Then proceed to adjust the gear-change mechanism as described in Chapter VI before finally tightening up the countersunk screws holding the casing.

Rear Transmission and Suspension. To strip down the rear transmission the brake drum must be removed first (*see* Chapter VI), then the brake shoes. The brake lever is held by a circlip which, when removed, allows the brake shaft to be knocked out with a drift. Before removing the brake lever—and this is important—mark its position so that when reassembled it will be in the same position as before.

The complete rear transmission is shown in Fig. 43. Disassembly is reasonably straightforward to reach the parts required, remembering that before the drive shaft can be pulled out second gear should be engaged

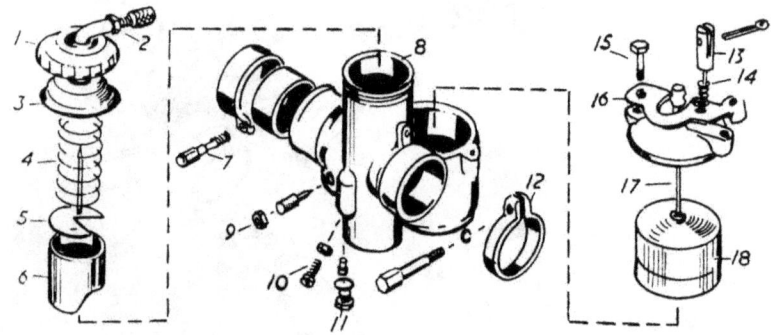

FIG. 44. STANDARD BING 1/20/22 CARBURETTOR

1. Locking ring for top cap
2. Cable adjuster
3. Top cap
4. Slide spring
5. Spring clip
6. Throttle slide
7. Pinch bolt
8. Carburettor main body
9. Pilot air screw
10. Throttle slide stop
11. Pilot jet assembly
12. Pipe clip
13. Tickler with yoke end
14. Tickler spring
15. Cover bolt
16. Tickler anchor plate
17. Float needle
18. Float

and the sliding gear, shaft, selector form and countershaft and top gearwheel removed. Take care not to lose any of the needle rollers.

The gear casing has only to be removed if the rear wheel drive has to be changed. This can be unscrewed and taken off together with the gearchange segments and the casing taken off together with its pressure spring and protection plate. If damaged, the drive casing together with the suspension, may have to be replaced completely as a service unit.

Points to note in reassembly are that the two rubber gaskets on the rear suspension bearing bush are properly located and that the bush does not turn during tightening (otherwise these gasket rubbers may be damaged). The suspension must not be overtightened so that it has no freedom of movement. After reassembling the rear brake, check that the brake lever points to the top. Finally tighten after the engine has been refitted in the frame.

When the complete rear drive unit to the engine is being reassembled a locating bolt can be used as a guide; press the gear casing against the engine and turn the brake drum to engage the gear wheels. Then tighten lightly with a flat washer, spring washer and nut on the locating bolt, followed by all the socket head screws. The long bolt fits on top of the flange. The rest of the assembly should then follow in logical sequence, consult Chapter VI for details of gear-change adjustment.

Removal of the drive shaft with shock absorber requires the knocking out of the dowel pin on the helical gear, and undoing the locking plate and slackening the left-hand nut to pull off the gear. The gear is then freed by tightening the nut slightly when it can be levered off. Remove grooved thrust washer and gear and the three balls with the driving plate. Remove hub and place the remaining assembly in a vice or strike with a rubber hammer to press out the driving shaft together with the dished springs, wire rings and thrust washer. Remove the key and flange cover complete with gasket and knock out the driving shaft and flange complete with bearing.

The rear spring can be disassembled by holding the barrel in a vice and unscrewing the support bracket. Remove counter spring and shock absorber rubber, then tighten the pull rod in a vice and unscrew the base with a special spanner. Remove inner and outer springs and disc, and finally the pull rod. Reassemble in reverse order, remembering to lock the support bracket, when finally tightened in place, with a centre punch. *See also* Chapter VIII and Fig. 49.

An exploded view of the carburettor is shown in Fig. 44. No special attention is called for, other than cleaning when required and adjusting for idling speeds. Recommended jet sizes, needle position and idling setting are as detailed in the specification in Chapter I.

CHAPTER VIII

PRIMA D, FURTHER DETAILS

A COMPLETE set of special tools for the Prima D is shown in Fig. 45. In addition there is also a bench stand with fixtures for holding the engine and rear transmission unit for a complete strip down. The purpose of the special tools is indicated as a guide to which are indispensable for a

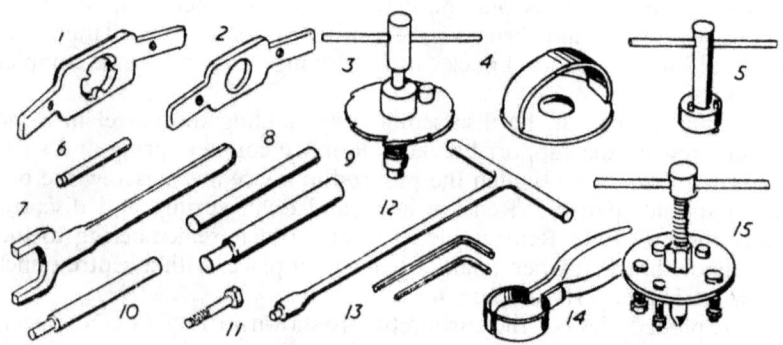

FIG. 45. SPECIAL TOOLS FOR PRIMA D

1. Support for clutch hub
2. Support for clutch bell
3. Clutch bell drawer
4. Clutch jig
5. Tool for rear wheel springing
6. Punch for removing brake adjuster
7. Spanner for upper bearing ring
8. Punch for connecting rod check
9. Mandrel for gudgeon-pin
10. Punch for fitting distance and bearing bushes
11. Extractor bolt
12. Socket spanner for housing screws
13. Allen keys
14. Piston ring pliers
15. Drawer for brake drum

complete maintenance job. Normally few, if any, of these tools would be of use to the average owner unless he wants to undertake complete overhauls, etc. Basically they are all concerned with engine stripping down and reassembly.

Front Hub. (*See* Fig. 46, *also* Fig. 29.) The front hub can be disassembled completely after removing the wheel from the frame and taking off the brake backplate. The axle can then be knocked out from the brake drum side with a block of hardwood or a rubber hammer. Then remove the spacer bushes, sealing rings and circlips. Tap out the bearings with a suitable drift.

When reassembling, the left-hand bearing is fitted first followed by the

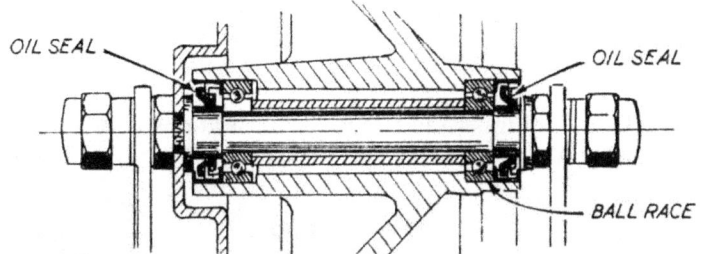

Fig. 46. Prima D Front Hub Section
Note positions of oil seals.

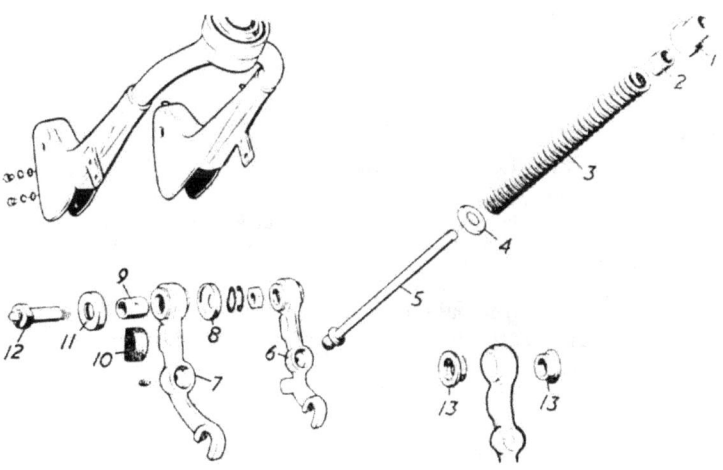

Fig. 47. Front Fork and Pivoted Link Assembly

1. Spring guide bush
2. Inner bush
3. Front fork spring
4. Cap
5. Spring guide rod
6. Right-hand pivoted link
7. Left-hand pivoted link
8. Cap
9. Spacer bush
10. Rubber buffer
11. Cap
12. Grease nipple
13. Bearing bushes

circlip. The spacer tube follows, when the right-hand bearing and circlip can be added. Both bearings should now be packed with grease. The spacer bushes are then inserted into the sealing rings and assembled, checking that the seals are the right way round—*see* Fig. 46. Replace the axle from the brake drum side and check that when finally in position it projects an equal amount each side.

Front Forks. (*See* Figs. 47 and 48.) The illustrations show the complete front fork assembly which can, if necessary, be dropped right out after

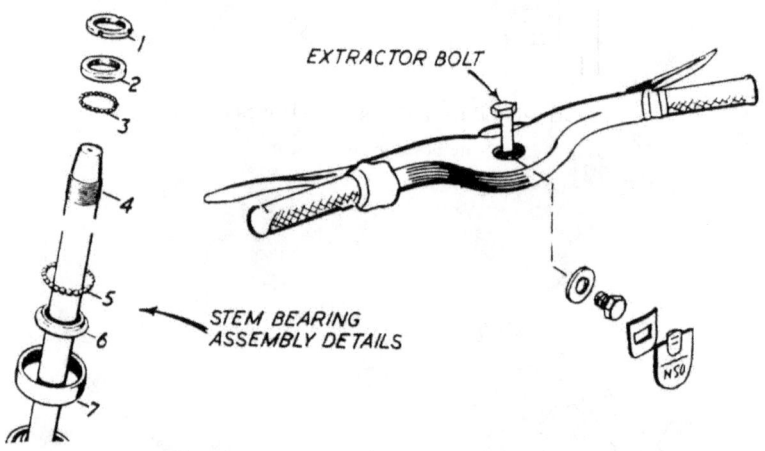

FIG. 48. FRONT FORK AND HANDLEBARS

1. Adjusting nut
2. Upper bearing cup
3. ¼-in. balls (35)
4. Front forks
5. ¼-in. balls (23)
6. Lower bearing cone
7. Ring for grease cup

first removing the handlebars (*see* later). Removal of the handlebars exposes the top end of the fork tube together with the upper bearing cup and adjusting nut. If a thin flat spanner is used to hold the bearing cup the adjusting nut can be unscrewed with a C-spanner. Then unscrew the bearing cup and the forks will drop free. At the same time the 35 ¼-in.-diameter balls in the upper steering head bearing will be freed and care must be taken not to lose them. Also the 23 ¼-in.-diameter balls in the lower steering head bearing must be collected. On reassembly the respective bearing cups are smeared with grease and the balls placed in them.

The extent to which the upper bearing cup is tightened and locked by the adjusting nut governs the "play" in the steering. When it is correctly set up there should be no play at all, but at the same time the forks must turn smoothly and easily from side to side.

If the steering head cones, cups and balls need attention or replacement the front fork cowling must also be removed, after dropping out the forks.

The races can then be knocked out of the head with a length of tube and the lower cone knocked off the fork stem with a punch applied from the bottom through the two holes.

The front springs can be removed by unscrewing the two small bolts on the underside of each front fork when the pivoted link can be pushed upwards slightly to remove the buffer. The pivot bolt holding the link can be knocked out, after the hexagon nut holding it on the inside has been removed and the link is removed complete with caps, bush, spring guide rod, etc. Consult the illustration for correct order of reassembly and be sure to include all washers and spring washers, where indicated.

If the bushes in the pivoted links require replacement the old bushes can be knocked out with a punch and new bushes pressed in. These will now require opening out to final size with a reamer so that they are a smooth, easy fit on the spacer bushes.

Handlebar Removal. The handlebars can be lifted by removing the cover plate (*see* Fig. 48) and rubber base plate and then unscrewing the hexagon-headed bolt with spring washer under. A pulling tool is specified for lifting the handlebars off, but this can usually be done by applying gentle force (but never hitting with a hammer). The handlebars should then be rested carefully on to a cloth laid on top of the machine, taking care not to strain or damage the cables, etc.

To remove the handlebars entirely it will be necessary to disconnect all four control cables at the handlebar end, remove the headlamp and dip-switch lead.

Speedometer and Speedometer Drive. To remove the speedometer drive it is necessary to remove the fork cowling, battery box, instrument panel and the edge strips on the right- and left-hand legshields, also the right-hand side panel. Remove the six nuts on the bottom of the legshield at the front and loosen the bolt on the swinging arm so that the speedometer drive shaft can be pulled out. Remove the rubber cap and unscrew the knurled nut on the speedometer. The speedometer drive can now be pulled out from the top, opening the cable clips slightly to free, if necessary. Replacement follows the reverse order.

Before the speedometer itself is removed the battery should be disconnected (i.e. remove the earth lead from its fixing bolt) to avoid any possibility of shorting. Through the door in the instrument panel, unscrew the knurled nut on the end of the speedometer drive to release the cable and pull out the three lamps complete in their holders. Unscrew the three round nuts and remove with the clips so that the speedometer can be lifted out from the top of the instrument panel.

Rear Springing. (*See* Fig. 49.) The rear wheel and hub must be removed to gain access to the rear spring fixing. If the circlip on the left-hand end of the bearing pin is then removed the pin can be driven out with a punch, when the rear spring unit will drop down. The pin should also be removed from the brake cam lever.

The bearing bush can be driven out with a bush, if a replacement is required, and the new bush pressed into place. This bush will then require reaming out to final size. Wear may also have taken place on the mounting holes in the transmission casing when it is recommended that these holes be reamed out to a suitable oversize dimension and a

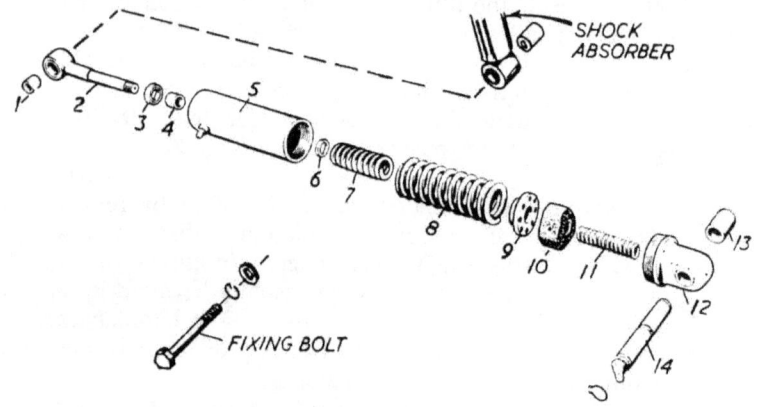

FIG. 49. REAR SPRING ASSEMBLY

1. Bearing bush
2. Pull rod
3. Sealing ring
4. Bearing bush
5. Spring casing
6. Washer
7. Inner spring
8. Outer spring
9. Base plate for pull rod
10. Rubber shock absorber
11. Spring stop
12. Connexion lug
13. Bearing bush
14. Bearing pin

larger bearing pin refitted, available as a standard spares item up to 15·5 mm diameter.

Fuel Tank. The fuel tank must be removed before the cylinder head or barrel can be removed with the engine still in the frame. First remove the sparking plug and then the tool box, held by a single mounting bolt and lock washer, detach the fuel pipe from the fuel tap, loosen the union nut holding the tap so that it can be turned to one side. Loosen the inlet air silencer and pull off. Disconnect the lead from the fuel gauge tank unit. The two bolts holding the tank can then be removed allowing the tank to be lifted out by twisting to the right.

If the tap is to be attended to, remove the split pin on the universal joint and push the control rod forwards. With the fuel line detached the tap should now unscrew. If the tap is leaking the cause may well be that the cork gasket has shrunk slightly due to the scooter's having been stored for some time in a warm, dry atmosphere. The tap may leak slightly when the machine is first used again but the gasket will soon swell to produce a proper seal. The same thing can happen when a new gasket is fitted.

Saddles. Saddle assembly is straightforward. No special attention should be required, with removal and fitting fairly obvious, except that a special tool is specified for compressing the spring so that the holding bolt can be screwed out.

Saddle covers should be washed in warm soapy water—a point often overlooked being that to keep the saddle clean minimizes the chances of clothing becoming soiled. An uncovered machine left standing for any length of time in a typical "town" or industrial atmosphere can collect an amazing amount of surface grime.

Body Panels. Disassembling and refitting the various body panels is fairly obvious, the main thing to watch being to replace the screws, etc., correctly, with appropriate washers underneath. The following table clarifies which other panels, etc., have to be removed first before a particular panel can be detached.

ITEM	TO BE REMOVED FIRST
(i) Side panels	Nothing (operate catches)
(ii) Front fork cowling	Headlamp, then two countersunk screws inside headlamp casing and four countersunk screws on rear of legshield
(iii) Front centre section panelling	Saddles, front luggage carrier bolts, side panels, fuel tap control rod, then four screws and nuts and rubber grummets
(iv) Legshields	Fork cowling, battery, battery box, instrument panel, legshield edge strips
(v) Front mudguard	Front wheel and front forks, then three bolts on inside of mudguard
(vi) Front bumper	Three bolts on inside of mudguard
(vii) Legshield edge strips	Remove three grub screws to detach
(viii) Footrests	Held by nuts (also one bolt securing silencer)

CHAPTER IX

THE PRIMA V AND III ENGINE

THE 174 c.c. Prima V and 146 c.c. Prima III engines are basically the same throughout, the difference being that the bore of the Prima III engine is reduced from 62 mm to 57 mm, thus accounting for the swept lower volume. The compression ratio is also modified, being 6·35:1 in the case of the 174 c.c. engine and 6·5:1 for the 146 c.c. engine. The same maintenance and stripping notes apply throughout.

The engine unit complete is shown in Fig. 50, mounting being by the single bolt. Since the engine unit is relatively easy to remove from the frame, and working on it is so much easier under these conditions, working on the engine *in situ* is not generally recommended. The following operations can, however, be carried out without removing the engine—

(i) Gearbox and rear wheel drive removal.
(ii) Cylinder head removal.
(iii) Cylinder and piston removal.
(iv) Gearbox and gear-change mechanism removal.
(v) Gear shaft bearings removal.
(vi) Clutch removal.

To remove the engine as a complete unit, the following items must be removed or detached first—

(*a*) both side panels and tank cap;
(*b*) rear wheel and rear-wheel mudguard, subsequently supporting the rear of the machine on blocks;
(*c*) spark plug;
(*d*) complete exhaust unit (from cylinder onwards);
(*e*) footrests (both sides);
(*f*) air induction flange;
(*g*) carburettor;
(*h*) disconnect electric wiring connexions—ignition coil lead, red, yellow and black leads on regulator and clamp, and starter cable from generator. The battery should also be disconnected by undoing the earth screw and removing the negative (earth) lead to prevent possible shorts;
(*i*) disconnect control cables at engine end—i.e. clutch cable and rear wheel brake cable;
(*j*) disconnect gear change rods.

The lower end of the rear shock-absorber can then be freed by removing the slotted screw and using a mandrel to drive off the lock plate on the lower bolt. The mandrel should be left in position. Remove nut and washers on the right-hand side of the engine mounting bolt and drive out with a suitable mandrel, supporting the engine whilst the bolt comes free. The engine is then free, except for the mandrel holding the rear wheel shock-absorber, which can now be pulled out. The engine can be mounted on a special stand (*see* Chapter X) for further work to be carried out on it, or merely laid on a bench and supported, as necessary.

The cylinder head is secured with four nuts and spring washers, two of which have small spacer tubes under. These correspond to the lower two

FIG. 50. THE COMPLETE ENGINE UNIT OF THE PRIMA V

positions when refitting. The cylinder barrel can be drawn off the four long studs, remembering or marking which way round it was fitted, exposing the piston. Gaskets are fitted at the top and bottom of the barrel, i.e. one head gasket and one crankcase gasket, and these must be replaced if damaged. The bottom gasket must be fitted the right way, i.e. with the cut-outs corresponding to the port openings in the cylinder barrel. The gudgeon-pin is located by two circlips, one at each end, which, when removed, allow the gudgeon-pin to be driven out with a suitable punch or mandrel. It is not necessary to heat the piston to free the gudgeon-pin, nor to refit.

The gear housing, complete with rear wheel drive, bolts directly to the engine crankcase and if the appropriate nuts and washers are removed around the periphery the rear unit can be lifted off complete. This exposes the clutch unit mounted in the crankcase.

To remove the clutch a special tool is required (*see* Chapter X) which fits on to the crankcase and is then screwed up to compress the clutch springs. The large circlip in front of the cup can then be removed with pliers and the pressure cup, springs and spring cups withdrawn.

A holding tool (*see* Chapter X) is then applied to the lined disc, the tab on the locking ring bent back, the nut unscrewed and the locking ring removed. The lined disc can then be withdrawn. Component parts of

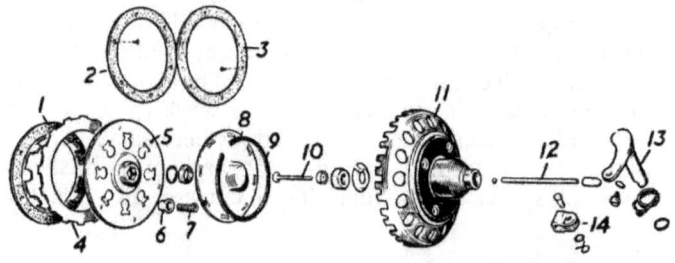

FIG. 51. PRIMA V CLUTCH

1. Thrust plate
2. Clutch plate
3. Clutch plate
4. Clutch plate
5. Main plate
6. Spring cup (8)
7. Spring (8)
8. Clutch cup
9. Circlip
10. Thrust rod
11. Damper
12. Thrust rod
13. Lever
14. Yoke

FIG. 52. THE DYNASTART UNIT ON THE PRIMA V AND III KL, SHOWING ALSO THE BATTERY POSITION IMMEDIATELY IN FRONT OF THE ENGINE

the complete clutch assembly are detailed in Fig. 51. When replacing the clutch the reverse procedure is adopted, first refitting the lined disc and supporting plate together with the spindle, replacing the locking ring and tightening the supporting plate up with the nut. Spring cups, springs and pressure cup are inserted and compressed by the special tool, enabling the circlip to be snapped in place.

THE PRIMA V AND III ENGINE

The generator assembly (Fig. 52) is removed from the front of the engine; first take off the fan housing, then the spring clip on the fan wheel releasing the cover. Bend locking washer tabs back to unscrew the central bolt, holding the crankshaft against rotation by locking the connecting rod—e.g. with a mandrel through the little end resting on blocks of wood. The fan can then be removed, tapping it with a block of wood to free, if necessary, but taking care not to damage the fins. Alternatively, use the technique described in Chapter VII for dismantling Prima D engine.

The dynamo unit is now exposed. The dynamo housing can be withdrawn after the four screws holding it have been removed, and the brushes

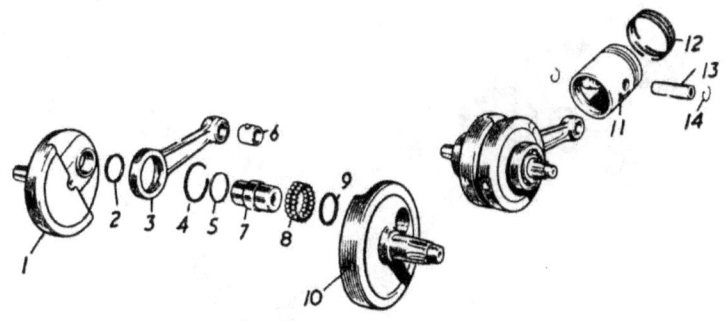

FIG. 53. CRANKSHAFT ASSEMBLY

1. Crankshaft
2. Washer
3. Connecting rod
4. Airclip
5. Race
6. Little end bush
7. Crank pin
8. Rollers (40)
9. Washer
10. Crankshaft
11. Piston
12. Piston rings (3)
13. Gudgeon-pin
14. Circlip (2)

pushed back, by using a pin and bolt inserted into the armature shaft. Finally remove the key on the crankshaft. A special extractor must be used to withdraw the rotor, which is rather a tricky operation as if either the rotor or crankshaft is damaged, the cost of replacement components will be high. The complete generator unit is shown in Fig. 63.

With the dynamo unit removed a mounting tool (*see* Chapter X) can be fastened to the front of the crankcase after the screws holding the crankcase halves together and the crank assembly complete with the rear end of the crankcase have been removed. The mounting tool is then replaced on the end of this half of the crankcase with four nuts and the crank assembly finally extracted from the crankcase half.

If bearings have to be replaced in the crankcase it is necessary to warm the castings to get them out, and also to refit the new bearings. Only moderate heating should be necessary, and preferably even heating applied all over the casting, so that the bearings may be withdrawn and replaced without having to force them in or out.

A complete and exploded view of the crankshaft assembly is shown in Fig. 53. This should provide adequate reference for reassembly, etc. Special notes regarding the reassembly of other main components are as follows—

Clutch, refit lined disc and supporting plate together to crankshaft, then replace lock plate, supporting plate with nut (using the holder). Tighten

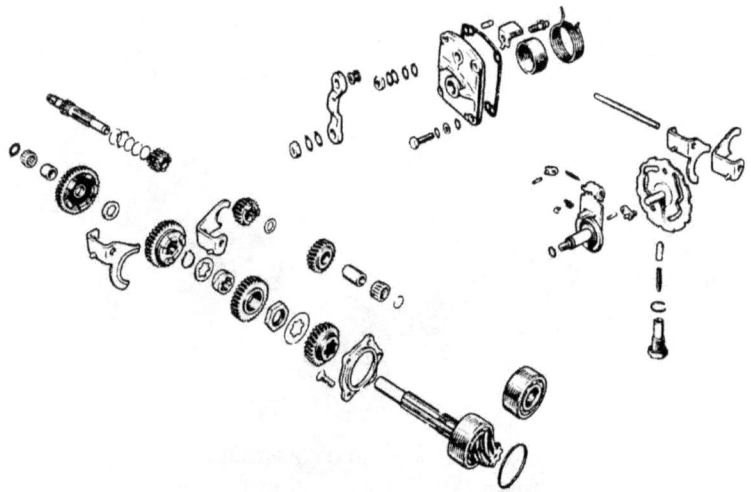

FIG. 54. COMPLETE GEARBOX COMPONENTS, THIS VIEW IS USEFUL FOR ESTABLISHING CORRECT ORDER OF REASSEMBLY

and secure nut. Insert spring cups and springs, fasten mounting tool to crankcase insert pressure cup and compress springs. Insert circlip.

Generator, the shaft taper should be free from grease and oil when replacing the armature. Replace in the reverse order to disassembly.

Piston, replace with cut-out facing exhaust port. Insert one gudgeon-pin circlip, then replace gudgeon-pin and finally second circlip. Oil gudgeon-pin and little end bush before refitting.

Cylinder, check that bottom gasket is the right way round. Oil piston and cylinder before reassembling.

The gearbox unit complete with rear wheel drive, as detached, exposes the damper wheel or clutch drum at the front end. Before disassembly the unit should be drained completely of oil. Then remove the rear wheel hub, plate and brake, the brake lever, return spring and spacer. Consult Fig. 54, for guidance on these parts.

Starting at the other end again insert a screwdriver through one of the holes in the damper wheel to bend back the locking washer, then unscrew the central nut and remove the wheel, together with its bush and locking plate. The gearbox can now be detached by removing the six holding screws on the intermediate housing and extracting this housing with a mounting tool, finally removing with a ring spanner. The remainder of the disassembly then follows logically, using an extractor, if necessary, to remove the spacer shim. The gearbox in exploded view is shown in Fig. 54.

When replacing gears, check that the pressure bolt is mounted the right way round (end pointing downwards). Insert gear selector plate and

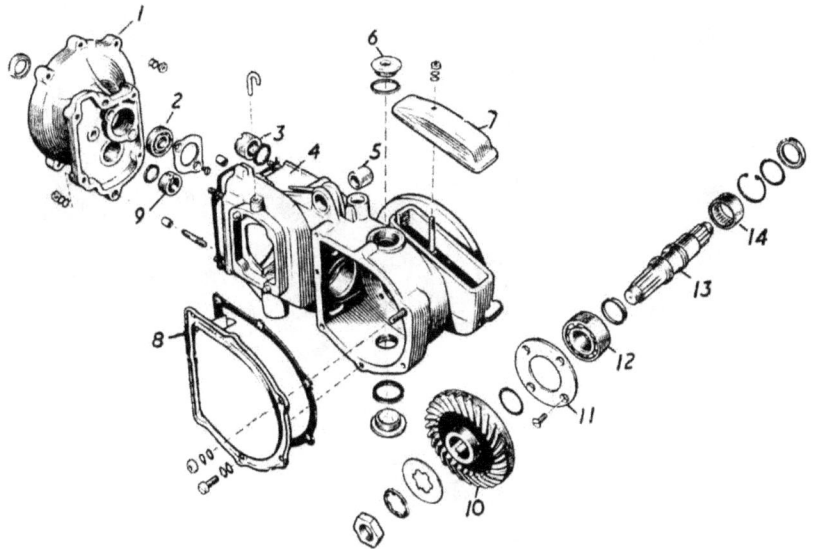

FIG. 55. PRIMA V REAR TRANSMISSION

1. Intermediate casing
2. Ball bearing
3. Outer race for needle rollers
4. Transmission casing
5. Bush
6. Oil filler and drain plug
7. Cover
8. Cover
9. Outer race for needle rollers
10. Pinion
11. Flange
12. Ball race
13. Spindle
14. Needle roller bearing

selector arm together so that the bore of the arm is in line with the bores in the plate. Then replace main shaft complete with selector fork and insert fork guide pin. Replace bush on driven shaft and third gear, with the three dogs pointing forwards. Secure check plate and check that gear play is of the order of 0·008–0·010 in. only—not more. Follow with the sliding gear (dogs pointing forwards). Insert selector fork and pin into proper place in the selector ring and properly fit the check plate—articulated edge facing rearwards. Insert first gear (wheel joint facing forwards) and check axle play in first gear, which should be 0·008 in. If greater than 0·012 in., shims must be used to take up the play. Finally, reassemble needle race and stick on gasket with grease.

In reassembling the gear-change assembly check that the catch of the gear arm lies between both ends of the spring. Refit gear lever in the central position between both stops and secure with a nut. Adjustment can be made, when completely assembled, by loosening the locking nut on the eccentric bolt and turning the bolt slightly one way or the other until proper engagement is obtained in all gear positions. This should

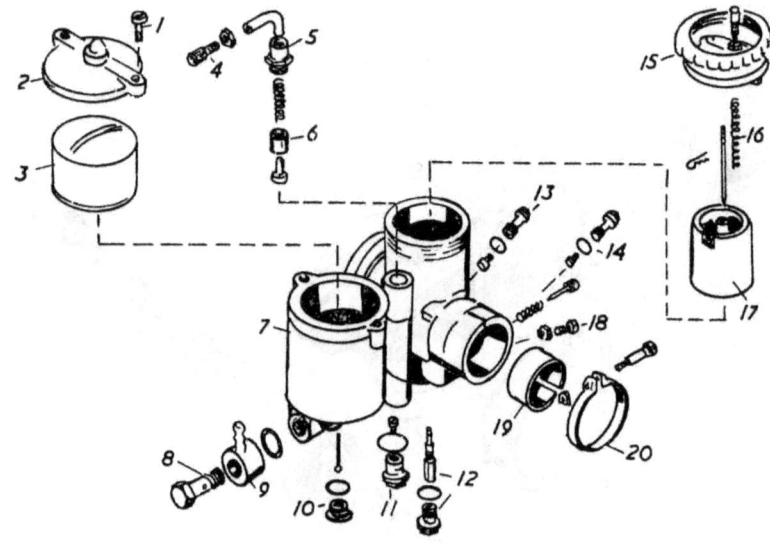

FIG. 56. PRIMA V CARBURETTOR

1. Screw
2. Float chamber cap
3. Float
4. Adjuster
5. Plug
6. Plunger
7. Body
8. Holding bolt
9. Swivelling hose adaptor
10. Float needle assembly
11. Plug and sealing ring
12. Plug, sealing ring and needle jet
13. Main jet assembly
14. Pilot jet assembly
15. Lock ring for top cap
16. Spring
17. Throttle slide
18. Screw and nut
19. Sleeve
20. Clamp

readily be audible in first, second and third positions, when turning the rear hub.

The complete rear transmission is detailed in Fig. 55. Dismantling follows after the gearbox. First unscrew the screws on the flange of the self-centring bearing. Then remove the cover for the driven shaft housing (held by slotted screws) and knock out the driven shaft with a soft hammer.

Replace the rear wheel hub and fit the mounting tool. Remove locking plate and nut and subsequently the crown wheel. Be careful not to damage or lose the shims behind the crown wheel. Finally remove flange from rear axle and drift out the axle bearing and intermediate ring. The split cone bearing is best pressed out in a vice, when after the gasket and sealing plate have been removed from the housing, and the circlip, the needle rollers can be knocked out. Reassembly follows the reverse order.

Carburettor parts are detailed in Fig. 56. The same comments apply as in Chapter VII, recommended jet sizes and settings again being given in the specifications in Chapter I. Note, however, that two different models of Bing carburettor may be fitted to the Prima V; also a slightly different model again is standard on the Prima III KL.

CHAPTER X

PRIMA V AND III, FURTHER DETAILS

SPECIAL tools for the Prima V and III are illustrated in Fig. 57, the purpose of the tools being noted in the caption. These are essentially concerned with engine stripping, etc., and are not necessary for ordinary maintenance work on the frame or simple engine overhauls like decarbonizing. Additional tools not shown include a stand for mounting the engine when removed from the frame, these being more in the nature of garage equipment for professional use.

Front Hub. To dismantle the front hub the wheel is removed as described in Chapter VI and the bearing tube knocked out with a suitable drift or mandrel. Remove the circlip holding the left-hand oil seal (speedometer drive already removed). The bearing tube and oil seal can then be knocked out from the other side and the process repeated on the right-hand side of the wheel. Consult Fig. 30 for details of the parts involved.

In reassembling it is important to check that the oil seals are mounted the right way round—lips on *both* sides facing *inwards*. The seal on the right-hand side should not be driven home completely flush with the hub but should protrude approximately one-sixteenth to one-eighth of an inch when finally assembled.

Front Forks. To remove the front forks first remove the front wheel, also the front fairing complete. The handlebars should then be detached (*see* later) and laid carefully on a rag on top of the assembly. The front brake cable should be removed, also the speedometer drive, then the speedometer drive shaft can be extracted. Detach the cable from the foglamp and release this cable completely from the clips holding it in the front mudguard. The upper bearing cup on the top of the fork stem can then be held with a thin flat spanner and the adjusting nut unscrewed with a C-spanner. Finally remove the bearing cup, when the forks will be free to drop downwards. At the same time take care not to lose any of the balls in the top and bottom bearings—35 $\frac{1}{8}$-in.-diameter balls in the top bearing and 23 $\frac{1}{4}$-in.-diameter balls in the bottom bearing.

Reassembly follows the reverse order: pack the bearing cups with grease to hold the balls, tighten the upper bearing cup and adjust ring until there is no play but the forks swing easily and smoothly to the full extent both ways. Consult Fig. 58 for details of the components involved.

If it is necessary to remove the bearing bushes, they can be knocked

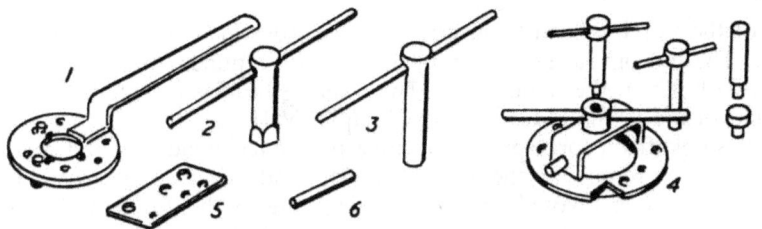

FIG. 57. SPECIAL TOOLS FOR THE PRIMA V

1. Support for clutch
2. T-spanner for driving shaft
3. Retaining spanner for driving shaft
4. Tools for dismantling and re-assembling clutch
5. Guide plate for driving shaft
6. Mandrel for connecting rod

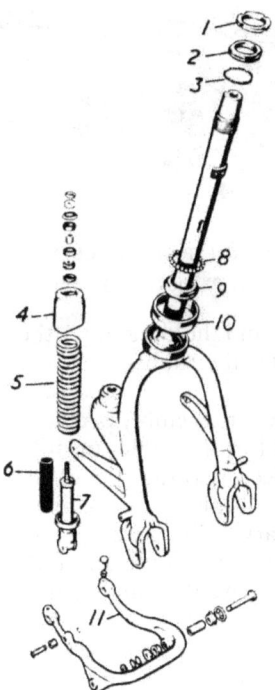

FIG. 58. FRONT FORK ASSEMBLY, PRIMA V AND III KL

1. Adjusting nut
2. Bearing cup
3. $\frac{1}{8}$-in. balls (34)
4. Tube
5. Spring
6. Tube
7. Shock absorber
8. $\frac{1}{4}$-in. balls (23)
9. Bearing cone
10. Ring
11. Leading links

out of the steering head by inserting a tube from each end and knocking free. The bottom race can be tapped free with a punch inserted through the two holes in the under side. The steering head is essentially similar to that of the Prima D described in Chapter VIII.

The single front fork spring is located on the left-hand side and can be detached by removing the wheel, fairing and front mudguard. The swinging arm is pivoted on two bearing pins with attendant bushes, washers and nuts (*see* Fig. 58). The bottom end of the shock absorber is attached to the swinging arm by a single pivot pin and bushing, locked on the inside with a circlip. The upper end of the shock absorber is

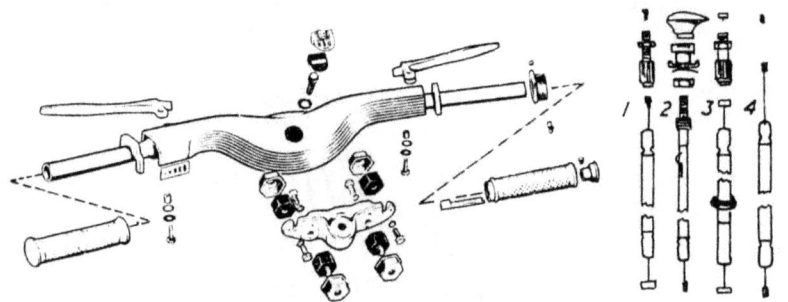

Fig. 59. Handlebar Assembly, Prima V
Cables are (1) clutch; (2) choke; (3) front brake; (4) throttle.

secured with a lock-nut and holding nut, the remaining components shown being retained under the rubber ring when the unit is withdrawn.

Handlebars. The handlebar assembly is detailed in Fig. 59. To remove completely, the brake and throttle cables must be detached, also the front cowling to detach the reflector so that the cable connectors for the blue, red and brown wires can be broken—checking against the wiring diagram when replacing, if necessary. The cover cap (bearing the coat of arms and NSU mark) is removed to locate the bolt holding the handlebars which, when unscrewed, allows the handlebars to be pulled off using an extractor bolt (*see* Fig. 48). Details for stripping the twist-grip control and levers are given in Chapter VI (*see* Figs. 35 and 36).

To remove the flexible handlebar attachment from the handlebars, remove the handlebars as above, and the dip switch. Unscrew the two front screws and loosen the two rear screws so that the handlebar attachment plate can be pressed out. Then unscrew the flexible rubber mountings. Refit in the reverse order, using a rubber hammer to knock the handlebar attachment plate back into place.

Speedometer and Speedometer Drive. The speedometer drive can be detached from the front wheel, after the wheel has been removed, simply by unscrewing the single nut and spring washer holding it in place. To obtain access to the speedometer head for removal the instrument panel must be released to swing back (the front fairing is removed first to gain access to the fixing screws). The instrument panel is held by two screws at the front and two screws with nuts and washers at the back of the legshield. The drive shaft is detached from the speedometer head by unscrewing the knurled nut when the instrument can be released by removing the two round nuts and clips leaving it free to be lifted out from the top, after first pulling the lamp and holder out of its socket.

During this operation the battery should be disconnected against possible shorting by uncoupling the earth lead from the frame.

Rear Springing. (Fig. 60.) In the rear-wheel suspension the engine unit is pivoted about the centre of the frame and sprung and damped by a single combined helical spring and shock absorber unit. This unit is pivoted to a lug on the rear gear casing and the upper end locating in a lug welded to the frame immediately behind the tank position. The rear mudguard must be taken off to gain access to the fixing points, also the clutch cable must be detached.

Remove the screw holding the bottom lock washer, then the washer and knock out the pin with a suitable drift. Loosen the lock-nut and nut on the upper bearing pin, pressing down on the front of the engine unit to relieve the load on these nuts.

The clutch lever should now be detached by unscrewing the screw holding it and withdrawing the lever from above. Lever the suspension to the rear again by pressing down on the wheel hub, unscrew the nut and lock-nut at the top of the shock-absorber unit and withdraw spring, shock-absorber, rubber plates and cups, etc. *See* Fig. 60 for a complete description of the parts.

Refitting requires a tool to compress the spring until the top of the shock absorber (threaded end) protrudes approximately $1\frac{1}{2}$ in. above the spring cup so that it can be refitted in position with the bottom bearing pin and the rubber plate, nut and lock-nut assembled before releasing spring tension.

Fuel Tank. To remove the tank the following items must be detached or removed first—

(i) rear wheel mudguard;
(ii) batteries;
(iii) tool box;
(iv) rear suspension, as above (support the rear wheel drive casing on a suitable block of wood or similar packing, if rear wheel is also removed).

The filter cock, fuel line to carburettor and the air filter should also be detached. Loosening the two screws on the frame and folding the rear

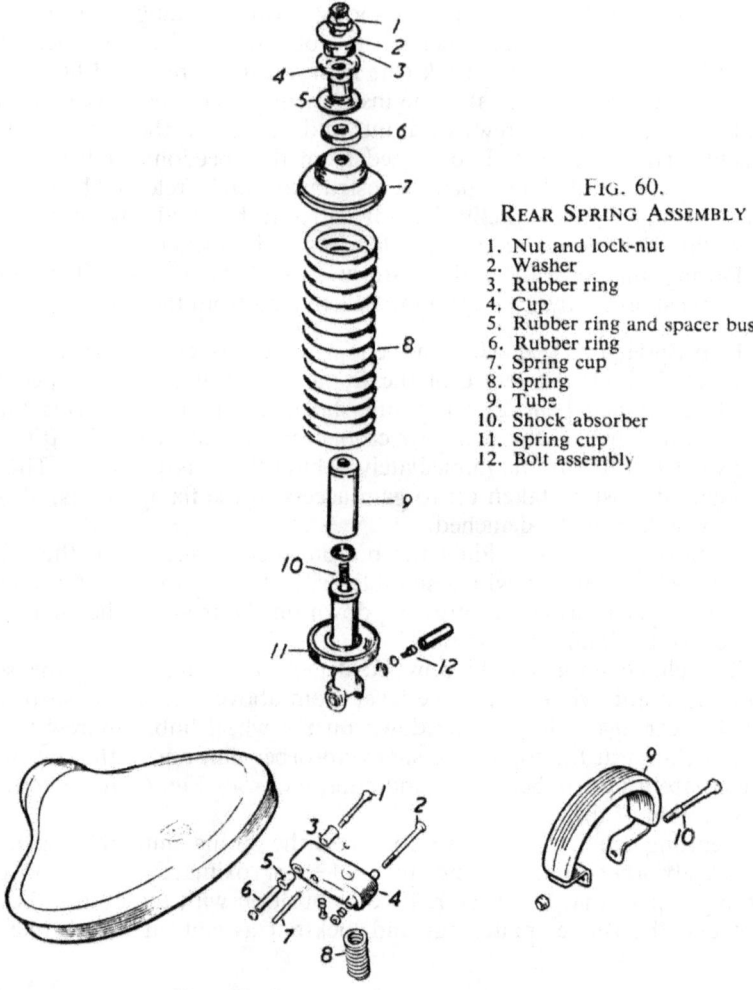

FIG. 60.
REAR SPRING ASSEMBLY
1. Nut and lock-nut
2. Washer
3. Rubber ring
4. Cup
5. Rubber ring and spacer bush
6. Rubber ring
7. Spring cup
8. Spring
9. Tube
10. Shock absorber
11. Spring cup
12. Bolt assembly

FIG. 61. PRIMA V SADDLE ASSEMBLY

1. Front bolt
2. Bolt
3. Bush
4. Saddle support
5. Bush
6. Spacer bush
7. Stop pin
8. Saddle spring
9. Handgrip
10. Rear bolt

end of the frame upwards should then allow the fuel tank to be removed from the left.

Replacement follows the reverse order, inserting the tank from the left and taking care to position the rubbers accurately. It is important that the tank is correctly aligned.

The filter cock embodies the fuel indicator and hence carries a plug-in electrical lead. If this is removed for any reason, or the cock is to be removed, the battery should be disconnected to avoid any danger of a short if the lead is laid on the frame. Removal and replacement of the filter cock should be obvious, although it is important to position it correctly when reassembling.

Saddles. The saddles (Fig. 61) are located by a stop pin secured by a spring clip. If this clip is removed and the saddle pressed down the stop pin can be driven out to the left with a punch. Pressing the saddle up then allows the saddle spring to be removed. Unscrewing the lock-nut and removing the expanding bolt then allows the saddle to be taken off.

On reassembly the saddle and grip are secured with the expanding bolt, the saddle pressed up and the spring inserted. Then press down on the saddle, insert the stop pin from the right and secure with its spring clip.

Stronger springs than standard are available, designed to give better support for heavyweight riders. To fit, simply follow the above procedure up to the point of removal of the spring and then the reverse sequence with the new spring in position.

Body Panels. The following table describes which panels, etc., have to be removed first before a particular panel can be detached.

Item	To be Removed First
(i) Side panels	Nothing, released by clips
(ii) Front fork fairing	Remove reflector; fairing is released by removing four countersunk screws and washers on rear side
(iii) Legshield	Batteries, fairing, instrument housing, footrests, horn, speedometer drive, legshield mouldings
(iv) Legshield mouldings	Held by three small screws
(v) Front mudguard	Remove front fork: mudguard is held by countersunk screws each side, and nut on clamp bracket. Remove mudguard upwards
(vi) Bumper	Held by two countersunk screws and bent over clamping tags
(vii) Rear mudguard	Remove rear wheel. Mudguard is held by one screw at front, two screws on the inside and one screw on the stay
(viii) Footrests	Held by screws and nuts

CHAPTER XI

THE DYNASTART UNIT

MOST small two-stroke engines employ a flywheel magneto to provide the necessary high tension (high voltage) electricity for supplying the spark at the sparking plug electrodes. The flywheel, in other words, is designed to act as a simple generator and the engine power absorbed in performing this additional function is negligible.

The principle of flywheel-magneto operation embodies a coil with two windings—a primary winding of relatively few turns and a secondary winding with a larger number of turns of thinner wire—a means of abruptly breaking the secondary circuit (the contact-breaker) and a condenser which serves to store up electricity and assist in delivering the high tension voltage as a powerful surge at the appropriate moment governed by the breaking of the circuit (i.e. the opening of the contact-breaker points). Thus the "timing" of the spark becomes, essentially, a matter of arranging that the contact-breaker points open at the correct moment. Since they are operated by a cam driven by the engine mainshaft it becomes a matter of correct circumferential *positioning* of the contact-breaker unit relative to the cam.

Since a flywheel-magneto is obviously an electrical generator the addition of a further coil to the same unit will provide an additional source of electricity for such auxiliary services as may be required—e.g. for battery charging or operating lights with the engine running. This takes no power from the magneto or "spark" circuit and is quite independent of it. At the same time it does not require any switching arrangement since it can operate continuously for the purpose it is required. The common flywheel-magneto, therefore, usually becomes a flywheel-magneto-generator.

The Dynastart unit carries this arrangement still further. Like the conventional flywheel-magneto-generator the Dynastart embraces an armature or rotating member carrying permanent magnets, a stator, contact-breaker and cam. Instead of separate poles for lighting and ignition supplies with their respective pole pieces, however, the stator consists of a large number of pole pieces, half of which carry starter windings and the other half shunt windings.

When driven by the engine the shunt windings are excited and generate current, both for lighting and ignition circuits. If, however, current is fed *to* the starter windings the unit operates as a series-wound motor, thus driving the engine for starting purposes. The circuit also embraces an

THE DYNASTART UNIT

ignition coil and condenser (for the high-tension spark supply to the plug), voltage regulator, cut-out and ignition starter switch. The generated voltage on the lighting circuit is limited by an automatic voltage control, remaining virtually constant and independent of engine speed. The cut-out switch closes at less than 12 volts to connect to the battery for charging.

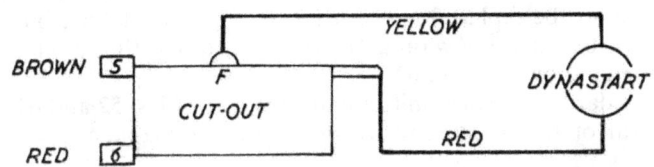

Fig. 62. Modification to Wiring on Prima D Using a Bosch Cut-out to Replace a Norris Unit

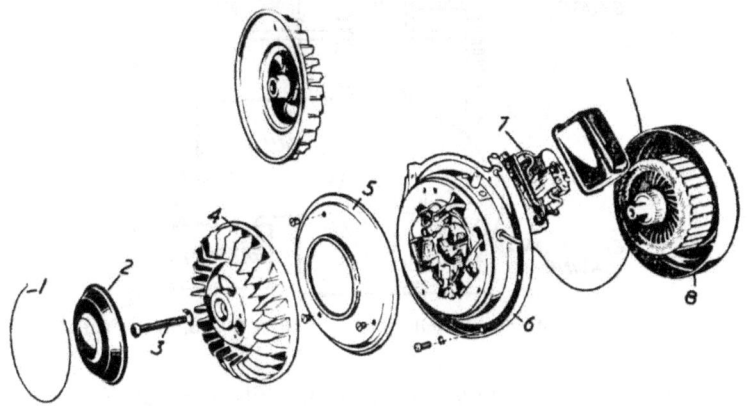

Fig. 63. Dynastart Unit, Prima V

1. Circlip
2. Cover plate
3. Bolt
4. Fan (incorporating automatic advance/retard mechanism)
5. Cover
6. Stator
7. Cut-out
8. Rotor unit

Normal no-load voltage is of the order of 15 volts but as current is consumed the voltage drops proportionately with output.

As far as the electrical side of the Dynastart unit is concerned, maintenance or repair is out of the question except for simple adjustments such as to the contact-breaker or ignition timing and replacing the carbon brushes. Faults which may develop within the unit itself can only be dealt with satisfactorily by a qualified specialist, although their occurrence should be rare.

The Prima D may be fitted with either a Bosch or Norris Dynastart unit. The Prima V has a Bosch Dynastart unit fitted as standard.

Although the two are essentially similar and some parts may be interchangeable the two makes should normally be regarded as *not* interchangeable as regards parts. The carbon brushes, for example, are definitely *not* interchangeable and so the type of unit must be specified in ordering spares. Nor can a Norris unit be used to replace a Bosch unit, although a Bosch Dynastart *will* fit as a replacement for a Norris unit. A Norris cut-out cannot be replaced (since it is no longer available), but a Bosch cut-out can be used *in lieu* on a Norris Dynastart with a modification to the wiring as shown in Fig. 62.

The standard Dynastart units are illustrated in Figs. 52 and 63. Details of removal of the whole unit are given in the chapters describing the

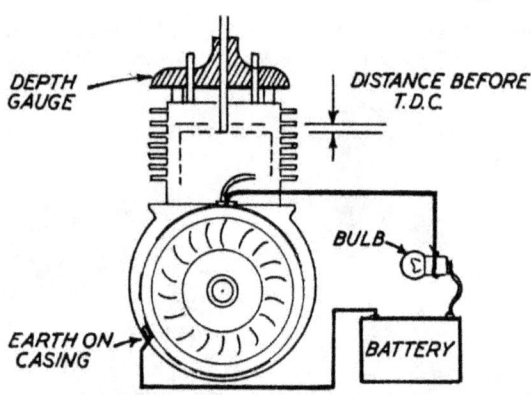

FIG. 64. TEMPORARY WIRING FOR CHECKING SPARK TIMING

respective engines (Chapters VII and IX), whilst contact-breaker adjustment is described in Chapter VI and Fig. 39.

Adjusting the Ignition Timing. The magneto unit incorporates an automatic advance and retard mechanism operated by centrifugal force. This is a simple spring loaded "trigger arm" mounted on the inside of the fan casing. For the purpose of setting up the correct ignition timing this arm must be held open, e.g. with a screwdriver. The timing position is then adjusted relative to the piston position in the cylinder by slackening the two screws holding the contact-breaker plate (*see* Fig. 39).

Checking is best done with the head removed, e.g. during final assembly of the engine after dismantling, but it can be done using a depth gauge inserted through the plug hole. If a battery is temporarily wired up as shown in Fig. 64 the point opening can be clearly established. The position of the contact-breaker base is adjusted, left or right as necessary, until the circuit is broken (i.e. the contact-breaker points have just parted, shown by the bulb going out) at a specified figure for the piston position

THE DYNASTART UNIT

before top dead centre position. This is 0·165 in.–0·170 in. before top dead centre in the case of the Prima D; and 0·177 in. before top dead centre in the case of the Prima V. The contact-breaker plate is then locked in this position by tightening the two screws, checking that this does not disturb the setting.

As an alternative to the lamp indicator, the opening of the points can be observed, although this is not a reliable method. A better scheme is to insert a piece of very thin, clean grease-free metal such as a 3-thou feeler gauge between the points and judge the opening position of the points by when this feeler gauge is no longer gripped securely and can be drawn out.

CHAPTER XII

IGNITION AND LIGHTING

WIRING diagrams for all models are given in Figs. 65, 66, 67. All Prima models except the III K and III KL employ a 12-volt electrical system, the battery in each case being two 6-volt 12-amp-hour batteries connected in series. The 6-volt electrical system on the Prima III K and III KL

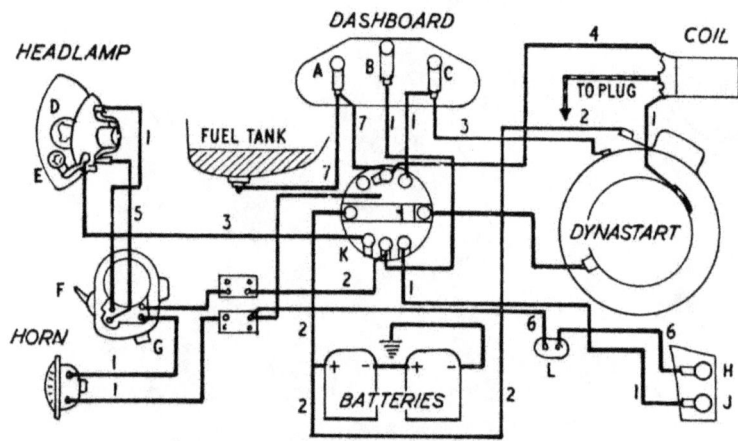

FIG. 65. WIRING DIAGRAM, PRIMA D

COMPONENTS
A. Fuel warning light
B. Speedometer bulb
C. Ignition warning light
D. Headlamp bulb
E. Parking light bulb
F. Dip switch
G. Horn button
H. Brake light
J. Tail light
K. Lighting-ignition switch
L. Stop light switch

COLOUR CODE
1. Black
2. Red
3. Brown
4. Yellow
5. White
6. Blue
7. Green

employs a single 6-volt 6·7-amp-hour battery. All wiring is colour coded, the coding being illustrated on the appropriate diagrams.

All wiring is assembled in the form of a cable harness—a single harness in the case of the Prima D and two in the case of the Prima V. The left-hand cable harness on the Prima V carries all the "live" wires and the right-hand harness the distributor wires. On the Prima III K and III KL

IGNITION AND LIGHTING

the circuit is simpler, except that the Prima III electrical system is similar to that of the Prima V but without the flasher unit.

When working on any part of the electrical circuit for replacement, etc. (except bulbs) it is generally advisable to disconnect the earth lead of the battery so that no shorts can be induced accidentally.

If necessary, the complete cable harness can be removed. Dip-switch wiring is a separate pair of leads running from the headlamp to the switch

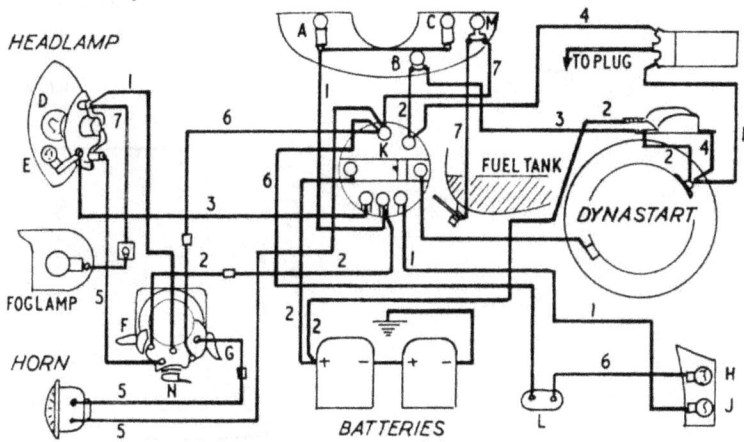

FIG. 66. WIRING DIAGRAM, PRIMA V

COMPONENTS	COLOUR CODE
A. Speedometer bulb	1. Black
B. Ignition warning light	2. Red
C. Clock light	3. Brown
D. Headlamp bulb	4. Yellow
E. Parking light bulb	5. White
F. Dip switch	6. Blue
G. Horn button	7. Green
H. Brake light	
J. Tail light	
K. Light-ignition switch	
L. Stop light switch	
M. Fuel warning light	
N. Headlight flasher switch	

(black and white leads on lamp terminals). If removed, the position of the two colours should be marked on the lamp socket for reference when replacing. The red, blue and brown leads running from the handlebar switch on the Prima V are joined with pull-apart cable connectors and if these are broken (e.g. for removing the switch) it should be noted that the brown lead from the switch reconnects to the white (horn) lead, the other two being reassembled colour for colour. The appropriate wiring diagram should be referred to, to clarify reconnexions, if necessary. The circuits are relatively simple and can be traced through quite easily with the wiring diagram as a guide.

Upon insertion of the ignition key on the instrument panel the ignition circuit is completed, indicated by the fact that the red warning light will come on. Pressing the ignition key down then closes the starter circuit, feeding the battery current to the Dynastart stator windings to make this unit operate as a motor and turn the engine over.

Turning the key to the first right-hand position (*see* Fig. 68) switches on the parking lamp and the headlamp and the tail light. Turning the key to the next position to the right switches on the twin-filament headlamp

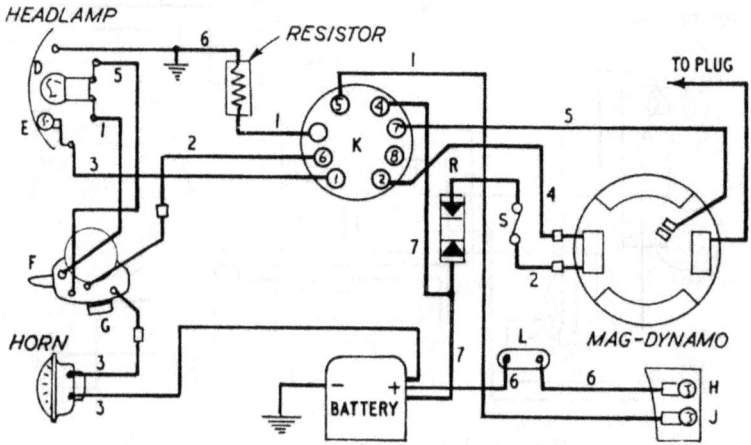

FIG. 67. WIRING DIAGRAM, PRIMA III K AND III KL

COMPONENTS

D. Headlamp bulb
E. Parking light bulb
F. Dip switch
G. Horn button
H. Brake light
J. Tail light
K. Light-ignition switch
L. Stop light switch
R. Rectifier
S. Fuse

COLOUR CODE

1. Black
2. Red
3. Yellow
4. White
5. Blue
6. ⎫
7. ⎬ Green

bulb and tail lamp. The dip switch (the top button on the left-hand handlebar switch) then controls the connexion of the second filament of the headlamp bulb. In the case of the Prima III KL the light switching is different, and the switch is mounted on the top of the headlamp cowling. Turning the switch to the left switches on the parking light, and to the right the headlamps.

On the Prima V a separate foglamp is also fitted. The switch for this is fitted on the left-hand side of the instrument panel but is wired through the dip-switch circuit. This switch will only close the circuit (i.e. switch the foglight on) with the main headlamp beam "dipped" by the dip-switch control. The Prima V also incorporates a headlamp flasher switch (marked red) on the back of the handlebar switch (*see* Fig. 6). This is a push-button control which enables the headlamp to be flashed on and off to signal other road users that you are intending to overtake, or that you are crossing a dark road junction, etc. Its use is actually rather limited for driving in this country.

The horn button (coloured green) is mounted on the underside of the handlebar switch on the Prima V, and on the rear face of this switch on the Prima D and Prima III. The horn is battery operated so that it will

FIG. 68. IGNITION KEY ALSO ACTS AS A LIGHT SWITCH, TURNING TO TWO POSITIONS TO RIGHT (PRIMA D AND V). FOG LAMP SWITCH (PRIMA V ONLY) IS ARROWED

operate without the engine running (as is necessary on some other scooters where the horn current is fed from the magneto generator coil). On the Prima D the horn itself is mounted in the front cowling behind the headlamp and can be reached by removing the headlamp. On the Prima V the horn is mounted on the back of the legshield underneath the instrument panel and the front fairing and instrument panel must be removed to gain access to it. On the Prima III KL the horn is in front of the engine—near the place occupied by the second battery on the Prima V.

The tail lamp housing incorporates a separate stop light actuated by a switch operated by the rear brake pedal. This switch is mounted close to the bottom pivot of the pedal under the footrest and is held by two screws and spring washers. The switch face is protected with a rubber cap, removal of which exposes the cables. If the switch is removed, its position must be checked on reassembly to ensure that it is operated fully by movement of the brake pedal.

The fuel-gauge indicator is wired to a warning lamp on the instrument panel which lights up when the fuel level in the tank has fallen to approximately $2\frac{1}{4}$ pints (Prima D) or $3\frac{3}{4}$ pints (Prima V and III). On the Prima D the gauge unit is screwed into the tank with the cable connexion protected by a rubber sleeve. On the Prima V the fuel-level gauge is incorporated

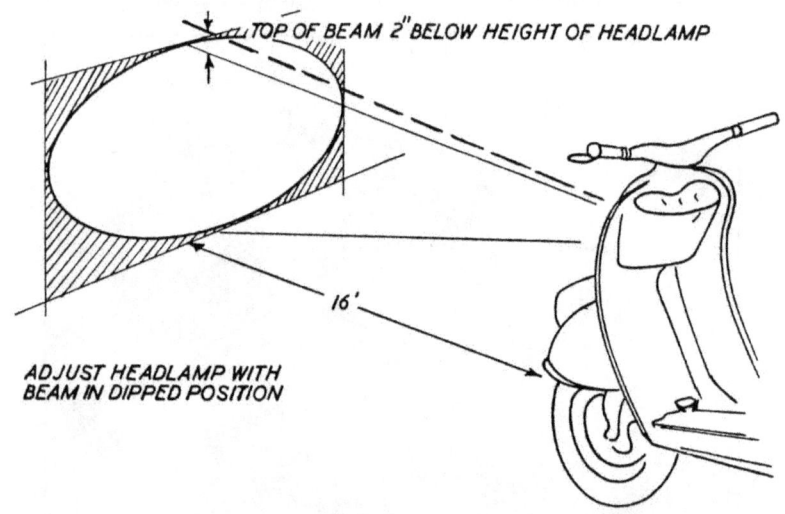

FIG. 69. CORRECT ADJUSTMENT FOR HEADLAMP BEAM (ALL MODELS)
When making adjustment, the rider should be sitting astride the machine.

in the filter cock attached with a cap nut. The cable connexion (green) simply plugs into a socket.

The headlamp on the Prima D can be adjusted by loosening the slotted screws at the top and bottom of the rim and repositioning as required. Recommended procedure for setting the beam is to place the scooter about sixteen feet from a wall or similar vertical surface, sit astride the machine in the normal riding position and adjust the lamp so that the top of the beam projected on the wall with the headlamp in the *dipped* position comes just below the vertical height to the centre of the headlamp (*see* Fig. 69). This latter height can be chalked or marked on the wall as a guide, if preferred, although it can usually be estimated by eye with sufficient accuracy. It is important *not* to adjust the dipped beam for any higher position as this will prove uncomfortable to other road users when driving at night. A common failing with scooter drivers, in fact, is to drive on the headlamp unnecessarily at night in well illuminated areas, to the discomfort of car drivers they may be following.

Headlamp removal on the Prima D simply involves removing the two screws loosened for adjustment, when the headlamp will come away. Disconnecting the spring then enables the bulb holder and bulb to be taken out, the parking light bulb being mounted in the reflector. The headlamp glass and reflector are removed by bending up the clips on the glass mounting ring and removing the glass, reflector, sealing ring and mounting ring as a unit. When replacing, make sure that the glass is replaced the right way up—word *oben* at the top; also the reflector—parking bulb at the top. Adjust the beam as necessary after refitting the lamp.

Headlamp adjustment and removal are essentially similar on the Prima V and III, the top position of the glass in this case being marked "this side up." On no account, on any model, should the reflector be cleaned by polishing as although it may be brought up brightly it will subsequently tarnish and the intensity of the beam will be reduced accordingly. The only satisfactory treatment for a tarnished or dulled reflector is to replace it.

When changing the fog-light bulb on the Prima V it is important to reassemble the right way round. The locking clamp on the light fitting must be inserted in the slot in the reflector with the larger spring pointing downwards as otherwise the locking clamp will touch the reflector and cause a short-circuit when the fog lamp is switched on. The fog lamp can be removed completely by taking off the front wheel, unscrewing the top and bottom screws on the lamp rim to withdraw the reflector assembly, disconnecting the cables and pulling out from below. A nut on the underside of the mudguard holds the lamp housing and, if removed together with its washer, enables the housing to be lifted off. For changing a bulb, of course, only the rim screws need be taken out and the reflector unit pulled forwards.

If it is necessary to remove the combined lighting-ignition switch from the dashboard it can be released by unscrewing the two countersunk screws on the switch, pushing the switch down into the glove locker and withdrawing it through the open locker. Lead connexions should be marked before disconnecting from the switch. Alternatively, check against the wiring diagram to establish the correct connexion for a lead which may have broken off.

In the case of the Prima V it will be necessary to free the instrument panel so that it can be tilted backwards to gain access to the ignition-lighting switch. Wiring can be examined in this position. If the switch is to be removed, unscrew the knob on the starter switch and remove the cover plate (held by a single countersunk screw). The two countersunk screws holding the switch can then be removed and the switch dropped free.

The combined tail light/stop light (double filament bulb) is fitted in a housing simpy attached to the rear mudguard. To remove, unscrew both countersunk screws and take off the protective caps. The tail light housing can be removed by unscrewing the two further screws and nuts holding it to the mudguard and disconnecting the cables. The blue lead connects to the stop light element and the black lead to the tail light.

Where replacement bulbs are called for in any part of the circuit only specified sizes and types should be used. Bulbs with higher wattage ratings will place unnecessary drain on the battery, without necessarily giving any better performance. Bulbs of lower rating may not give a satisfactory—or even legal—performance (minimum rating for the tail lamp bulb, for example, is 5 watts). Complete bulb specifications are—

Prima D

    headlight: 12 volt 35/35 watt
    parking light: 12 volt 2 watt
    tail light: 12 volt 5 watt
    brake light (stop light): 12 volt 15 watt
    speedometer bulb: 12 volt 2 watt
    clock dial bulb: 12 volt 2 watt
    fuel-warning light: 12 volt 2 watt

Prima V

    headlight: 12 volt 35/35 watt
    parking light: 12 volt 2 watt
    tail light: 12 volt 5 watt
    brake light (stop light): 12 volt 15 watt
    speedometer bulb: 12 volt 2 watt
    clock dial bulb: 12 volt 2 watt
    fuel-warning light: 12 volt 2 watt
    fog lamp: 12 volt 35 watt

Prima III KL and III K

    headlight: 6 volt 25/25 watt
    parking light: 6 volt 2 watt
    tail light: 6 volt 5 watt
    brake light (stop light): 6 volt 15 watt
    fuse in rectifier circuit: 2·5 amps.

INDEX

ADJUSTMENT, headlamp, 98
Air filter, 35
Alignment of gear change, 58

BATTERY, 21, 25, 46, 78, 94
Battery care, 44, 46
Brake cables, 55
Brake linings, 51, 52 *et seq.*
Brakes, 44, 51
Braking, 24
Body panels—
  Prima D, 75
  Prima V, 89
Bosch cut-out, 91
Bosch Dynastart, 91
Bulb specifications, 100

CABLES, 55
Cable harness, 95
Carburettor, 3, 4, 5
Carburettor—
  Prima D, 60, 68
  Prima V, 82
Changing gear, 26–7
Changing speeds, 17
Changing wheels, 48, 49
Choke, 10, 21, 22 *et seq.*
Clock, 30
Clutch, 4, 5, 43
Clutch—
  Prima D, 53 *et seq.*
  Prima V, 55, 77, 78, 80
Clutch cables, 55
Colour code, 94, 95, 96
Colour schemes, 6
Contact breaker, 61
Contact-breaker adjustment, 61
Cornering, 30
Crankshaft—
  Prima D, 64
  Prima V, 79

DECARBONIZING, 62
Dip switch, 12, 97

Distribution, 3
Driving technique, 25 *et seq.*
Dynastart, 10, 78, 90 *et seq.*

ELECTRICAL circuits—
  Prima D, 94
  Prima V, 95
  Prima III KL, 96
Engine—
  Prima D, 7, 63 *et seq.*
  Prima V, 9–10, 77 *et seq.*
Engine faults, 42 *et seq.*
Engine group, 7, 9–10, 63, 77
Engine lubrication, 32
Engine performance, 14

FAULT finding, 41 *et seq.*
Filter cock, 87
Final drive—
  Prima D, 8, 67, 68
  Prima V, 81, 82
Flywheel (*see* Magneto)
Fog lamp, 12, 96, 99
Forks—
  Prima D, 50, 52
  Prima V, 84, 85, 86
Frame, 7
Front brake—
  Prima D, 50
  Prima V, 52
Front hub, 70, 71, 84
Front wheel—
  Prima D, 50
  Prima V, 52
Fuel capacity, 101
Fuel mixture (*see* Petrol-oil mixture)
Fuel tank, 74, 87
Fuel tank level, 18
Fuel tap, 18, 19
Fuse, 96, 100

GEARBOX, 14, 65, 66 *et seq.*
Gearbox lubrication, 34, 35, 38, 40
Gear change, 12, 43

Gear-change cable adjustment—
   Prima D, 58
   Prima V, 60
Gear-change cables, 58
Gear ratios, 4, 5

HANDLEBARS, 9, 10, 30, 72, 86
Handlebar lock, 31
Handlebar removal, 73
Headlamps, 12, 97
Headlamp adjustment, 98, 99
Horn, 97
Horsepower, 15

IGNITION circuits (*see* Electrical Circuits)
Ignition switch, 11, 12, 21, 96, 97, 99
Ignition timing, 4, 5, 92
Instruments, 10

JACKING stand, 18
Jets (*see* Carburettor)

KICKSTARTER, 24

LAYING up, 62
Lighting bulbs, 100
Lights, 10, 12, 97
Lubrication—
   Prima D, 34 *et seq.*
   Prima V, 35 *et seq.*
   Prima III, 35 *et seq.*

MAGNETO, 91 *et seq.*
Maintenance and spares, 3
Maximum speed, 6
Maximum speed in gears, 17
Monthly lubrication, 36, 37
Monthly maintenance, 39

NEW machines, 33, 40
Noise, 43
Norris dynastart, 91 *et seq.*
NSU (Great Britain) Ltd., 3

OIL for engine (*see* Petrol-oil mixture)
Oil for lubrication, 36, 40

PARKING, 31
Parking lights, 12, 44

Petrol-oil mixture, 7, 20, 32
Plug gap, 60
Prima models—
   D, 8
   V, 1
   III, 2
   differences, 1–3
Prop stand, 18
Push starting, 24

REAR spring—
   Prima D, 69, 73
   Prima V, 87, 88
Rear transmission—
   Prima D, 67, 68
   Prima V, 81, 82
Rear wheel—
   Prima D, 52
   Prima V, 53
Recharging battery, 48
Rectifier, 96
Replacement bulbs, 100
Road speeds, 16
Routine maintenance, 37 *et seq.*
Running in, 33
Running-in speeds, 33

SADDLES—
   Prima D, 75
   Prima V, 88, 89
Spare wheel, 51
Spark plug, 60
Special notes, Prima D, 39
Special tools—
   Prima D, 70
   Prima V, 85
Specifications—
   Prima D, 3
   Prima V, 4
   Prima III, 5
Speedometer, 73, 86
Speedometer drive, 73, 86, 87
Stability, 30–1
Starter, 22, 44
Starter control cable, 57, 58
Starting, 21 *et seq.*
Starting troubles, 24
Steering head, 72
Stop light, 99 (*see also* wiring diagrams)
Stopping, 31

INDEX

Suspension, 7, 29
Switches, 11, 12, 96

TANK, 74, 87
Tank filler, 18
Throttle cable, 57
Timing (*see* Ignition timing)
Timing check, 92
Tools, 45
Tools, special—
  Prima D, 70
  Prima V, 85
Torque, 15
Twist grip, 56, 57
Tyres, 4, 5

Tyre changing, 50
Tyre pressures, 34, 35

USE of gearbox, 16, 28

WEEKLY lubrication, 36
Weekly maintenance, 39
Weights, 4, 5
Wheels, 4, 5, 48, 50 *et seq.*
Wheel change, 48, 49
Wiring colour code, 94, 95, 96
Wiring diagrams—
  Prima D, 94
  Prima V, 95
  Prima III KL, 96

AUTOBOOKS WORKSHOP MANUALS

ALFA ROMEO GIULIA 1300, 1600, 1750, 2000 1962-1978 WSM
BMW 1600 1966-1973 WSM
BMW 2000 & 2002 1966-1976 WSM
BMW 2500, 2800, 3.0 & 3.3 1968-1977 WSM
BMW 316, 320, 320i 1975-1977 WSM
BMW 518, 520, 520i 1973-1981 WSM
FIAT 1100, 1100D, 1100R & 1200 1957-1969 WSM
FIAT 124 1966-1974 WSM
FIAT 124 SPORT 1966-1975 WSM
FIAT 125 & 125 SPECIAL 1967-1973 WSM
FIAT 126, 126L, 126 DV, 126/650 & 126/650 DV 1972-1982 WSM
FIAT 127 SALOON, SPECIAL & SPORT, 900, 1050 1971-1981 WSM
FIAT 128 1969-1982 WSM
FIAT 1300, 1500 1961-1967 WSM
FIAT 131 MIRAFIORI 1975-1982 WSM
FIAT 132 1972-1982 WSM
FIAT 500 1957-1973 WSM
FIAT 600, 600D & MULTIPLA 1955-1969 WSM
FIAT 850 1964-1972 WSM
JAGUAR E-TYPE 1961-1972 WSM
JAGUAR MK 1, 2 1955-1969 WSM
JAGUAR S TYPE, 420 1963-1968 WSM
JAGUAR XK 120, 140, 150 MK 7, 8, 9 1948-1961 WSM
LAND ROVER 1, 2 1948-1961 WSM
MERCEDES-BENZ 190 1959-1968 WSM
MERCEDES-BENZ 220/8 1968-1972 WSM
MERCEDES-BENZ 220B 1959-1965 WSM
MERCEDES-BENZ 230 1963-1968 WSM
MERCEDES-BENZ 250 1968-1972 WSM
MERCEDES-BENZ 280 1968-1972 WSM
MG MIDGET TA-TF 1936-1955 WSM
MINI 1959-1980 WSM
MORRIS MINOR 1952-1971 WSM
PEUGEOT 404 1960-1975 WSM
PORSCHE 911 1964-1973 WSM
PORSCHE 911 1970-1977 WSM
RENAULT 16 1965-1979 WSM
RENAULT 8, 10, 1100 1962-1971 WSM
ROVER 3500, 3500S 1968-1976 WSM
SUNBEAM RAPIER, ALPINE 1955-1965 WSM
TRIUMPH SPITFIRE, GT6, VITESSE 1962-1968 WSM
TRIUMPH TR2, TR3, TR3A 1952-1962 WSM
TRIUMPH TR4, TR4A 1961-1967 WSM
VOLKSWAGEN BEETLE 1968-1977 WSM

VELOCEPRESS AUTOMOBILE BOOKS & MANUALS

ABARTH BUYERS GUIDE
AUSTIN-HEALEY 6-CYLINDER WSM
AUSTIN-HEALEY SPRITE & MG MIDGET 1958-1971 WSM
BMW 600 LIMOUSINE FACTORY WSM
BMW 600 LIMOUSINE OWNERS HAND BOOK & SERVICE MANUAL
BMW ISETTA FACTORY WSM
BOOK OF THE CARRERA PANAMERICANA - MEXICAN ROAD RACE
COMPLETE CATALOG OF JAPANESE MOTOR VEHICLES
CORVAIR 1960-1969 OWNERS WORKSHOP MANUAL
CORVETTE V8 1955-1962 OWNERS WORKSHOP MANUAL
DIALED IN - THE JAN OPPERMAN STORY
FERRARI 250/GT SERVICE AND MAINTENANCE
FERRARI 308 SERIES BUYER'S AND OWNER'S GUIDE
FERRARI BERLINETTA LUSSO
FERRARI BROCHURES AND SALES LITERATURE 1946-1967
FERRARI BROCHURES AND SALES LITERATURE 1968-1989
FERRARI GUIDE TO PERFORMANCE
FERRARI OPP, MAINTENANCE & SERVICE H/BOOKS 1948-1973
FERRARI OWNER'S HANDBOOK
FERRARI SERIAL NUMBERS PART I - ODD NUMBERS TO 21399
FERRARI SERIAL NUMBERS PART II - EVEN NUMBERS TO 1050
FERRARI SPYDER CALIFORNIA
FERRARI TUNING TIPS & MAINTENANCE TECHNIQUES
HENRY'S FABULOUS MODEL "A" FORD
HOW TO BUILD A FIBERGLASS CAR
HOW TO BUILD A RACING CAR
HOW TO RESTORE THE MODEL 'A' FORD
IF HEMINGWAY HAD WRITTEN A RACING NOVEL
JAGUAR E-TYPE 3.8 & 4.2 WSM
LE MANS 24 (THE BOOK THAT THE FILM WAS BASED ON)
MASERATI BROCHURES AND SALES LITERATURE
MASERATI OWNER'S HANDBOOK
METROPOLITAN FACTORY WSM
MGA & MGB OWNERS HANDBOOK & WSM
OBERT'S FIAT GUIDE
PERFORMANCE TUNING THE SUNBEAM TIGER
PORSCHE 356 1948-1965 WSM
PORSCHE 912 WSM
SOUPING THE VOLKSWAGEN
TRIUMPH TR2, TR3, TR4 1953-1965 WSM
TUNING FOR SPEED (P.E. IRVING)
VEDA ORR'S NEW REVISED HOT ROD PICTORIAL
VOLKSWAGEN TRANSPORTER, TRUCKS, STATION WAGONS WSM
VOLVO 1944-1968 ALL MODELS WSM
WEBER CARBURETORS (EMPHASIS ON ALFA & FIAT)

BROOKLANDS BOOKS & ROAD TEST PORTFOLIOS (RTP)

AC CARS 1904-2009
ALFA ROMEO 1920-1933 ROAD TEST PORTFOLIO
ALFA ROMEO 1934-1940 ROAD TEST PORTFOLIO
BRABHAM RALT HONDA THE RON TAURANAC STORY
BUGATTI TYPE 10 TO TYPE 40 ROAD TEST PORTFOLIO
BUGATTI TYPE 10 TO TYPE 251 ROAD TEST PORTFOLIO
BUGATTI TYPE 41 TO TYPE 55 ROAD TEST PORTFOLIO
BUGATTI TYPE 57 TO TYPE 251 ROAD TEST PORTFOLIO
DELAHAYE ROAD TEST PORTFOLIO
FERRARI ROAD CARS 1946-1956 ROAD TEST PORTFOLIO
FIAT 500 1936-1972 ROAD TEST PORTFOLIO
FIAT DINO ROAD TEST PORTFOLIO
HISPANO SUIZA ROAD TEST PORTFOLIO
HONDA ST1100/ST1300 PAN EUROPEAN 1990-2002 RTP
JAGUAR MK1 & MK2 ROAD TEST PORTFOLIO
LOTUS CORTINA ROAD TEST PORTFOLIO
MV AGUSTA F4 750 & 1000 1997-2007 ROAD TEST PORTFOLIO
TATRA CARS ROAD TEST PORTFOLIO

VELOCEPRESS MOTORCYCLE BOOKS & MANUALS

AJS SINGLES & TWINS 250cc THRU 1000cc 1932-1948 (BOOK OF)
AJS SINGLES 1955-65 350cc & 500cc (BOOK OF)
AJS SINGLES 1945-60 350cc & 500cc MODELS 16 & 18 (BOOK OF)
ARIEL 1939-1960 4 STROKE SINGLES (BOOK OF)
ARIEL LEADER & ARROW 1958-1964 (BOOK OF)
ARIEL MOTORCYCLES 1933-1951 WSM
ARIEL PREWAR MODELS 1932-1939 (BOOK OF)
BMW M/CYCLES R26 R27 (1956-1967) FACTORY WSM
BMW M/CYCLES R50 R50S R60 R69S (1955-1969) FACTORY WSM
BSA BANTAM (BOOK OF)
BSA ALL FOUR-STROKE SINGLES & V-TWINS 1936-1952 (BOOK OF)
BSA OHV & SV SINGLES - 250cc 1954-1970 (BOOK OF)
BSA OHV & SV SINGLES 1945-54 250-600cc (BOOK OF)
BSA OHV SINGLES 350 & 500cc 1955-1967 (BOOK OF)
BSA PRE-WAR MODELS TO 1939 (BOOK OF)
BSA TWINS 1948-1962 (BOOK OF)
BSA TWINS 1962-1969 (SECOND BOOK OF)
CATALOG OF BRITISH MOTORCYCLES (1951 MODELS)
DOUGLAS PRE-WAR ALL MODELS 1929-1939 (BOOK OF)
DOUGLAS POST-WAR ALL MODELS 1948-1957 FACTORY WSM
DUCATI 160cc, 250cc & 350cc OHC SINGLES FACTORY WSM
HONDA 50 ALL MODELS UP TO 1970 INC MONKEY & TRAIL (BOOK OF)
HONDA 90 ALL MODELS UP TO 1966 (BOOK OF)
HONDA MOTORCYCLES 125-150 TWINS C/CS/CB/CA WSM
HONDA MOTORCYCLES 250-305 TWINS C/CS/CB WSM
HONDA MOTORCYCLES C100 SUPER CUB WSM
HONDA MOTORCYCLES C110 SPORT CUB 1962-1969 WSM
HONDA TWINS ALL MODELS 125cc THRU 450cc UP TO 1968 (BOOK OF)
HONDA TWINS & SINGLES 50cc THRU 305cc 1960-1966 (BOOK OF)
INDIAN PONYBIKE, BOY RACER & PAPOOSE ILL PARTS LIST & SALES LIT
J.A.P. ENGINES 1927-1952 & MOTORCYCLES 1934-1952 (BOOK OF)
LAMBRETTA ALL 125 & 150cc MODELS 1947-1957 (BOOK OF)
LAMBRETTA LI & TV MODELS 1957-1970 (SECOND BOOK OF)
MATCHLESS 350 & 500cc SINGLES 1945-1956 (BOOK OF)
MATCHLESS 350 & 500cc SINGLES 1945-1966 (BOOK OF)
NORTON 1932-1947 (BOOK OF)
NORTON 1938-1956 (BOOK OF)
NORTON DOMINATOR TWINS 1955-1965 (BOOK OF)
NORTON MODELS 19, 50 & ES2 1955-1963 (BOOK OF)
NORTON MOTORCYCLES 1957-1970 FACTORY WSM
NORTON PREWAR MODELS 1932-1939 (BOOK OF)
NSU PRIMA ALL MODELS 1956-1964 (BOOK OF)
NSU QUICKLY ALL MODELS 1953-1963 (BOOK OF)
RALEIGH MOPEDS 1960-1969 (BOOK OF)
ROYAL ENFIELD SINGLES & V TWINS 1937-1953 (BOOK OF)
ROYAL ENFIELD SINGLES 1946-1962 (BOOK OF)
ROYAL ENFIELD 736cc INTERCEPTOR FACTORY WSM
ROYAL ENFIELD 250cc & 350cc SINGLES 1958-1966 (SECOND BOOK OF)
SUNBEAM MOTORCYCLES 1928-1939 (BOOK OF)
SUNBEAM S7 & S8 1946-1957 (BOOK OF)
SUZUKI 50cc & 80cc UP TO 1966 (BOOK OF)
SUZUKI T10 1963-1967 FACTORY WSM
SUZUKI T20 & T200 1965-1969 FACTORY WSM
TRIUMPH PRE-WAR MOTORCYCLE 1935-1939 (BOOK OF)
TRIUMPH MOTORCYCLES 1937-1951 WSM
TRIUMPH MOTORCYCLES 1945-1955 FACTORY WSM
TRIUMPH TWINS 1956-1969 (BOOK OF)
VELOCETTE ALL SINGLES & TWINS 1925-1970 (BOOK OF)
VESPA 1951-1961 (BOOK OF)
VESPA 125 & 150cc & GS MODELS 1955-1963 (SECOND BOOK OF)
VESPA 90, 125 & 150cc 1963-1972 (THIRD BOOK OF)
VESPA GS & SS 1955-1968 (BOOK OF)
VILLIERS ENGINE (BOOK OF)
VINCENT MOTORCYCLES 1935-1955 WSM

PLEASE VISIT OUR WEBSITE
www.VelocePress.com
FOR A DETAILED DESCRIPTION
OF ANY OF THESE TITLES

www.ingramcontent.com/pod-product-compliance
Lightning Source LLC
Chambersburg PA
CBHW070559170426
43201CB00012B/1883